AM I DOING THIS RIGHT?

AM I DOING THIS RIGHT?

LIFE LESSONS FROM THE ENCYCLOPEDIA BRI-TANYA

TANYA HENNESSY

ALLEN&UNWIN

SYDNEY · MELBOURNE · AUCKLAND · LONDON

This edition published in 2019
First published in 2018

Allen & Unwin
83 Alexander Street
Crows Nest NSW 2065
Australia
Phone: (61 2) 8425 0100
Email: info@allenandunwin.com
Web: www.allenandunwin.com

A catalogue record for this book is available from the National Library of Australia

ISBN 978 1 76087 556 5

Internal design by Romina Panetta
Set in Sabon LT Pro by Bookhouse, Sydney
Printed in Australia by McPherson's Printing Group

10 9 8 7 6 5 4 3 2 1

Hey there—I'm professional dancer/day-drinker/amateur psychic Tanya Hennessy.

Welcome to my book.

(I am dying . . . I wrote a book, it's here . . . you're reading it.)

This mess from Newcastle, who is constantly sweaty for no reason, who rarely washes her hair and rotates between the same four tops, wrote a goddamn book.

First up, I must admit I found this book hard to write. Because . . . it's a book. It' s not a radio break or a quick internet video. This is a book. The real deal. My words and stories are immortalised in it. For someone who overthinks dinner, the thought of that alone is terrifying.

I have put stuff in and taken stuff out countless times. I have overthought some pieces for months and, conversely, written other pieces in two minutes. I have no 'writing process' and I have no real idea what I'm doing. (I think that's normal. No one ever really does.) I'm just hoping what I'm doing is right . . . and I guess that's the crux of what this book is about.

Am I doing this right?

I died when I got an email from Allen & Unwin, asking me to write a book. It has been a lifelong goal, so to be sitting here, writing an intro to one, is surreal.

Even though writing a book was a major goal, I never thought I would get the opportunity to do it. I really didn't. I never expected to amount to much—even though I always wanted to.

Please know that I am genuinely honoured and grateful that I have been able to do this. Thank you for buying this book. It means the world to me. Sincerely.

I'm actually crying as I write this because a) I can't believe I did it . . . it's here! and b) because I really want Subway cookies and I don't want to put pants on and leave the house again.

I originally had the idea of alphabetising my thoughts and experiences when I was in high school, as something to do for a stand-up show, and then again, when I was 25, as subject matter for a cabaret (originally to be titled *Encyclopedia Bri-tanya: A kebabaret, a night of mixed meat and song.* This night WILL happen . . . when I find a tzatziki sponsor). Anyway, when I was approached to write a book . . . I knew this was what it had to be.

'So, what is this book about, Hennessy?' I hear you ask.

Great question—it's partly a memoir, and it's some jokes and observations, short anecdotes, lists, a bit of advice and a lot of swearing (sorry in advance). I wanted to create something different and something that was authentic. And that's what I've written. It's not linear, it's not conventional; it's not normal—but I hope you like it.

In short, it's sorta autobiographical but mainly it's relatable lols.

All the pieces are quick and easy to read. (That is, except for the first story, which goes for 7000 words, because I needed to get the book's word count up.)

What I'm saying is categorised by the letters of the alphabet, and if you want, you can dip in and out of it in between other, more important, things you're probably doing, like posting Insta stories.

I am genuinely worried about sharing this book with the world. I've told stories here that I have never told publicly before.

- It's about growing up and not wanting to.
- It's about questioning everything.
- It's about being a woman.
- It's about being a person.
- It's about asking yourself hard life-related questions.
- It's about anxiety.
- It's about comparing yourself to others.
- It's about social media.
- It's about truth.

It's about success . . . but, more importantly, it's about failure. I feel like the biggest lessons I've learned came from my biggest failures.

And, man, I've failed a lot.

This book will, hopefully, make you laugh and make you cry. I hope it will ultimately make you feel less alone, and maybe even inspire you.

So, lower your expectations, strap yourself in and enjoy.

TANYA X

BEFORE WE START, HERE ARE 10 FACTS ABOUT ME

- I can't read analogue clocks. Seriously.
- I'm nothing like my siblings. My brother and sister are both gym junkies and bodybuilders. And I like to sit. Once I was flirting with a guy (in my single days) and he saw my phone screensaver, which showed my sister and me . . . and he asked for her number.
- I didn't realise what carpenters do till I was 29. I figured they laid carpet, until one day I thought: *Wait, wasn't Jesus a carpenter? They wouldn't have had carpet when he was around. Or did they have a few Carpet Courts?*

- I applied to be Miss Newcastle Showgirl in 2008 and got rejected when they found out I had lied about having 15 years of Latin dance experience.
- I sit down in the shower. I'm a shower sitter. I probably have so many diseases.
- Joel Edgerton hit on me once and I rejected him—*WHYYYYYYY*?
- I still sleep with my childhood teddy bear, Morris. Well . . . he is a 'reinbear', half reindeer, half bear. I got him for Christmas when I was eight. I actually asked Santa for a real reindeer. I'm still pissed off I got this hybrid bear. This isn't what I wanted, Jan.
- I was almost a high school teacher. *Seriously*. I have a degree in theatre and half a Dip. Ed. in secondary teaching. I've thought about finishing it but I honestly don't know if I can teach real live children when there are videos of me on the internet talking about my boob hairs.
- Many people think the best musicals are *Les Misérables* and *The Phantom of the Opera* but I truly believe the best musical ever is *High School Musical 2*.
- I used to be a stilt walker at Luna Park in Sydney. The first day I learned to walk on my stilts at Luna Park, I stumbled, and, fearing I was going to fall, grabbed someone's head for balance. It was Russell Crowe's head. He was not pleased.

PREVIOUSLY, ON TANYA HENNESSY

You know the phrase 'When I grow up, I want to be a ...'? Well, when I was a kid, I finished that sentence with the word 'actor'. (Full disclosure: I still say 'When I grow up, I want to be a ...', even though I am a fully formed adult. Apparently.)

From a very young age, I wanted to be an actor. We're talking from when I was, like, three or four years old. But even then, I think I knew, deep down, that it wouldn't work out for me.

Mainly because I couldn't act.

(I watch back scenes of me acting and, honestly, they're offensive to the eyes and several other senses. To those who have seen them, I sincerely apologise.)

In retrospect, I feel like one of those bad singers auditioning for *Australian Idol* (Vintage Reference) who has a really supportive family, so nobody has ever told them how bad they are, and they find out when they perform and the judges are like, 'Are you kidding with this?'

I was one of those super-annoying kids. Surprised? I was that child who would put on a show and charge their parents to watch. Why my parents and their friends actually paid, I'll never know.

My shows started off consisting of me singing 'Part of Your World' from *The Little Mermaid*, then escalated to full productions. Scenes, other songs, dancing, a puppet show. These would be 45-minute shows, a lot of which was improvised dance.

They would have been a punishment to watch.

When I got older, I upgraded my shows to include the kids in my neighbourhood, and would organise rehearsals with them. I would make programs, make tickets, coordinate the costumes. The annual Christmas show was an event, until there was an actual show stopper, when the parents of the kids in my shows told me I wasn't making the experience fun. I was told, 'Tanya, the kids are sad because you're yelling at them a lot.' Well, if those kids had nailed the kick ball change and their upstage entrances, maybe I wouldn't have needed to yell.

I would have been, like, eight at this point. I just loved performing. I took it so seriously. Too seriously.

I started drama classes at the local children's theatre school when I was nine or 10. Apparently, my mum called them about me taking classes when I was two and they were like, 'Nah, if she can't talk, she can't do drama.' The thing was, I *could* talk. I talked before I walked. #gifted

While the other kids at my primary school did sport as their extracurricular activity, I did singing and drama. I have never played a ball sport in my life. Seriously. In fact, I don't know the rules of any sport.

So, when I was in Year Six and preparations for the annual school musical, *A KIDsummer Night's Dream*, rolled around, I was desperate for a role.

I was one of the only kids who did drama outside of school. I was gunna nail this.

I didn't.

Well, I kinda did. I was cast as fairy 34. However, every kid who wanted to be in the show could be, so I was more or less just making up the numbers.

I wore a skin-tight yellow unitard (with wings, obviously) that was, unfortunately, see-through. My 12-year-old bee-sting boobs were horrifically visible. Thank god I couldn't keep up with any of the choreography; this meant I was moved to the back and so only a very special few could see my nips.

For some reason, that experience made me hungrier to be on stage. I decided that I wanted to go to a performing arts high school, so I auditioned for the Hunter School of the Performing Arts, I got in . . . and I went. It was the best school. I loved it.

They let us do all kinds of crazy stuff you probably couldn't do at a normal high school. When I was 15, I directed a play with a friend from the year above me. We did it all ourselves— raised the money to put it on, organised to get the rights, cast it, booked the theatre, did a press release. We asked a NIDA set designer to do the set for us. It was the Fucking Real Deal. In the end, we made a ton of money, but the principal told us we had to 'reinvest it' in the school, which was disappointing, as we wanted to 'reinvest it' in inflatable furniture and hair mascara.

Then I graduated from high school, and I really don't know how I did, given that in Year 10 I got four per cent in a maths test. Seriously.

I went to Charles Sturt University, to do a degree in theatre (and media). The university's in Bathurst, which was a town of 30,000 people and 5000 of them were uni students—it was wild.

Funnily enough, at the time I was so sure I was going to be an actor that I paid people to do the projects for my media subjects. Why would I need media subjects when I was going to be an actor? A theatre actor, what's more.

'Can you do my documentary video? I'm not ever gunna need to film or edit, so I'll just pay you to do my assignment.'

'Can you do my website? There's no way I'll need to know how to make a website.'

'Can you do my radio assessment? I'll never work in radio, anyway. I hate it. It's all ads.'

Seriously, all of that happened. What an idiot. But, apart from being an ignorant dick about my media subjects, I loved uni. I did so much performing there and I honestly couldn't believe I got to do exactly what I wanted for three years.

Once, in an improv class, our lecturer told us to pick an animal to pretend to be for an hour. I looked at those who chose frogs (too much jumping) and flamingos (too much standing on one leg) and felt nothing but raw pity for them. I myself had chosen to be a sloth, and for the better part of 60 minutes, I slept off a midweek hangover *and* it was noted that I was the most committed to this exercise out of every member of the class.

At Charles Sturt, I also played an albino pub owner, a sperm and, very convincingly, a tree. It was all so experimental and off the wall. My major work had a Freudian theme and all of us in it were basically nude. I regret inviting my parents to that one, not to mention my 10-year-old brother.

When I finished uni, I did some drama teaching, and went overseas and did some stage-managing at the Edinburgh Fringe Festival. I was still desperate to be an actor, even though I had zero idea of the best way to make this happen. So, when I returned to Australia, I got a job stage-managing musicals in Sydney. The shows I was a stage manager for included *Tell Me on a Sunday* and *Little Women: The Musical*.

I'd figured I'd be close to the action, and that, by some miracle, a brilliant casting director would see me lifting a piano or a desk or whatever, point her finger and say, 'Her! She's the woman we need for this show!'

This did not happen. For *Little Women*, I had to wait behind the curtain while the female lead sang her big note before the interval, when the lights went from bright and blinding to darkness. My job was to grab her and take her backstage before the lights came up again, because it took so long for her eyes to adjust that she couldn't get off the stage quickly enough. The irony that I was busy getting someone *off the stage* when all I wanted to do was get *on the stage* was not lost on me.

After that, I quit stage management, having decided to *really* focus on performing. So, naturally, I went for the job at Luna Park in Sydney as a clown and stilt walker. This was problematic because, honestly, I struggle walking just on the ground. I sometimes danced in the stage shows too. You know those 'shows' that are basically a whole lot of actors in plush character suits parading down the street dancing to Venga Boys songs and waving at children. Kind of like a pov Disneyland. Yep, I danced in those. Not well, but I did it. To this day, I believe that having been paid to dance makes me a professional dancer.

I got an agent, who found me no work (but was hot AF). I did a NIDA short course in presenting, and I did an acting-for-camera course at Screenwise in Surry Hills. I did a lot of Co-Op/Pro-Am shows which is industry slang for unpaid but, because I have an ego and a degree, I don't wanna say 'unpaid'.

I was broke as, and did more stage-managing—even though I hated it—to get by. I was reliant on Centrelink for a bit (read: for a lot) because I wasn't booking any gigs, and Luna Park only needed me on Friday, Saturday and Sunday nights. There was a time when I earned so little money that I couldn't afford to get my car registered, so would have to walk to Centrelink and get lifts to Luna Park. (Strangely enough, I always seemed to be able to afford Mars Bars.)

I probably went to 150-plus auditions when I lived in Sydney and was trying to 'make it' as an actor. I heard that, statistically, for every 40 castings you go for, you get one. That statistic wasn't true for me. As an 'actor', I would go to three to five castings a week. When you go to a casting, the holding room, where you wait with the other actors, is usually as small as a teenager's bedroom, and full of people who look like you, which is confronting. Being in one is not fun at the best of times, let alone when you're desperate. And I was desperate.

I just wanted to book one job.

Firstly, to prove to my parents I could do it.

Secondly, to prove to myself I could do it.

Thirdly, so I could afford to get my car registered. When you've been rejected more than 150 times, it's hard to go into a casting room. You want the gig so badly that you stress out, and don't get it because you're stressed. It's such a vicious cycle and so difficult to break.

When will someone say yes to me? I got to the point where I didn't believe this would ever happen, because I hadn't heard 'Yes' for such a long time. When you only hear 'Unfortunately, no' or 'Sorry' for years, you can't help but doubt yourself. I was doubting myself, my ability, my everything. Things were starting to feel so hopeless. I was close to giving up and working in a bank.

I wanted to perform so badly, and I just needed a chance. For one person to see something in me and give me an in.

Eventually, I booked one job as a prostitute in an opera. It was a French opera, and I was basically covered in dirt with no shoes, and wearing an ill-fitting corset. I was suspended above the stage in a giant cage for a grand total of three minutes.

Then, in 2011, I got a job working for Disney. I was a dresser on *Mary Poppins* at the Capitol Theatre in Sydney at night, and, during the day, I was the warm-up comic/audience wrangler on a kids' TV show called *Pyramid*. This involved playing my ukulele and telling terrible kid jokes.

But during this time, I had an epic breakdown. I was suffering the worst migraines I'd ever had, and needed to go to hospital. I started on antidepressants. I wasn't coping at all.

I knew I couldn't keep putting tap shoes on the show's stars and sitting in the shadows—and I reckon my body was telling me that. It was telling me that I had to stop working backstage. For good. The money I made being a dresser was incredible but it's never been about the money for me. It's about the work. I have to create. And then something happened. One day, during a quick change, one of the women in the ensemble cast mentioned that I'd be good at radio. Probably because of my persistent need to banter. I am allergic to silence (which is not so helpful backstage). While I liked doing stand-up in some ways, I also found it really hard: what I wanted was someone to bounce off.

Radio, hey? I had never seriously thought of that.

After a few weeks spent googling courses and calling different schools, like the Australian Film, Television and Radio School and the Western Australian Academy of Performing Arts, I fucked off the idea of going back to school and cold-called a radio station in Newcastle. They said that I could volunteer there. *YES*.

It was December 2011. I was 26 and I'd just left my well-paying job in Sydney (not to mention giving up my dream of being an actor) to live with my parents, make no money and volunteer at a radio station. I knew only one thing: *this had to work out*. I knew I had to give it everything. So, I gave it everything. I had a new goal now. *National radio*.

I went into the radio station at 4 a.m. five days a week, to watch the breakfast show being done and learn how it all worked. At weekends, I came in to learn 'the panel' and then, after a few months, I was asked to do 'mid–dawns'. This is the midnight to 5 a.m. shift, when nobody but lonely truckies, shiftworkers and my best friends would be listening.

A few months after being asked to do mid–dawns, I was offered a paid producing role. This wasn't instead of the mid–dawns. It was as well as. So, I would do the midnight to 5 a.m. shift, have a coffee, and then produce the brekky show from 6 a.m. to 10 a.m. Then I would pass out.

The first time I was live on air, I was so nervous. My voice was shaking. I was shaking. I sounded like I might burst into tears at any second. And the buttons! So many buttons. Plus, the phone was ringing with people calling in with their random stories and I had no idea how to get them on the air or if I was even on air myself.

Then I got the chance to do weekend shifts on air too, and, because I am a complete nutjob, I took it. For a while there, I worked crazy hours, seven days a week, for such bad money I'm too embarrassed to reveal it here.

I worked hard. Really fucking hard. Having produced the brekky show (7 a.m. to 9 a.m.), I then did an on-air stint from 9 a.m. to 2 p.m. I was exhausted, so I drank a lot of coffee. And because I drank a shitload of coffee, I needed to pee *a lot*. At one point, I went to the toilet during a song and left a fader down. *Oops*. Nothing went to air for five minutes. *Fuck fuck fuck*.

Then I did it again, another time. I wish I could tell you I didn't do it a third time, but . . . yeah, no. I got demoted.

I went back to producing, which I liked, but I'd had a taste of being on air and, goddamn, I wanted more of it.

I put the feelers out to another network, one of Australia's biggest radio companies. I wanted to be at one of their stations, NXFM—it was the station I grew up listening to. Everyone knew it and loved it. It was the sound of Newcastle.

So, I emailed the generic station email, butterflies in my stomach as I typed. I didn't think they would even read my email. If they did, I didn't think they would bother with me: I wasn't experienced enough. But I got a reply, saying they would meet with me. I should have been pronounced legally dead because, yeah, I died.

I met with the then content director, and I was so nervous and desperate, I even wore make-up to the meeting. As soon as I set foot in that building, I knew this was where I had to be.

He asked me to give him two weeks to find a place for me, and, even then, it would only be casual work, panelling shifts. *Who cares?* He could have asked me to clean the toilets and I would have asked him to pass the Ajax.

I looked at my phone every five minutes during that two weeks. Every time, there was nothing. Until—obviously—I was getting my first-ever pap smear.

'So sorry,' I said to the doctor who was busy inspecting me with a plastic duck bill, 'but I have to take this.'

The content director was calling!

'Hi, Tanya,' he said. 'Can you talk?'

'Sure,' I told him. With my knees up and a woman aged in her 40s looking into my vagina.

'Great,' he said. 'I've got a casual job for you.'

Yes.

For the next three months, I worked my arse off at NXFM. I was panelling the drive shows, and by panelling I mean I was inserting the traffic reports, and making sure the ads didn't run over the program. At first, it was Fifi Box and Jules Lund, and then Dan Debuf and Maz Compton. (I would go on to co-announce with both Jules and Dan, nationally. If you'd told me at the time that would happen, I would have died all over again.)

I wasn't allowed to be on air during the day (when people listened), but that was okay. I did the mid–dawns again, and I tried so hard. (Too hard, looking back.) The feedback I got was pretty harsh, but I needed it: I got better.

Finally, I was put on weekends. *Yes!!!*

A few months into my time at the station, I was asked if I wanted to audition for the breakfast spot in Griffith. Griffith? Ah, no thank you. I'd already gone back to Newcastle, which I'd thought was as regional as it would get for me. But . . . breakfast. Wow. I *really* wanted to do breakfast. So I moved to Griffith.

It was amazing. I was doing breakfast radio! I mean, I didn't know what I was doing. Like, I didn't have a clue. So I just made it up as I went along. And you know what? It turned out pretty . . . okay. It felt right. People were calling in and I would talk to them and we were connecting, and *I was doing radio like a real radio person!*

After eight months, I was asked if I would like to leave the small smoke of Griffith for the comparatively bigger smoke of Toowoomba, in Queensland. There, I was paired with a cool dude named Hamish—he'd been on air for 15 years and generously showed me the ropes.

After 18 months in T-ba (as it's known), I got the call to move to Canberra. It was 4 January 2016. It was hard at the start—really hard. My co-announcer, Ryan, and I were bullied. We were taking over from a well-loved, long-running show, and people weren't happy. (More on this later.) But once we warmed up, we were making some pretty good radio. Or we thought so, anyway.

This was when I really started to get involved with making my videos. When I started, I had someone else filming and editing them, but then I was like, *Nah, I can do this myself.* And you know what? It was once I started doing my own thing that I really began to get some traction. So much so that in February 2017, one of my videos—'Realistic Make-up Tutorial'—was viewed 250 million times. I know. I couldn't believe it.

Some of the people who could believe it, weirdly enough, were the casting agents who'd rejected me all those years ago. Suddenly they were knocking on my door, asking me to audition for this and be a part of that. I got approached by US management people, and I went to New York and LA in July 2017, to meet some managers and casting agents.

Tanya's diary
13 July 2017

I wish you could be inside my head right now.

I'm in a backlot of Formosa at the Lot in West Hollywood. I've been cleared by security (twice) and walked to the building (the wrong one, twice)—met the receptionist, talked too much. Now, I'm here.

I have been told I'm 45 mins early—which is a first, 'cause I'm a mess and always late.

I'm sitting downstairs out of the building in the 43-degree weather because I feel so stupid for turning up so bloody early. Like I know they are already off me. I look too keen.

The building I'm sitting in front of is OWN and Harpo Studios, which is also next to the building of Funny or Die, Will Ferrell's digital company that has 15 million likes on Facebook. They created Drunk History *and* Between Two Ferns *and it's the best digital comedy company in the world.*

As I sit here, writers are walking past me with their note-pads, people are moving sets and props, actors are walking around with costumes and sunglasses. It's not how I thought it would be. People are just working; yes, it's Hollywood but it's just work for everyone on this lot.

A guy has walked out in a Funny or Die tracksuit. Again. It's 43 degrees. He's loudly talking on the phone about casting. He is pacing and he looks at me while I adjust my fucking underwire. I am literally wearing a bra I have owned for seven years. It does not fit. It's a C and I'm now an E. It's really gross under the shirt.

As I sit here in La-La Land in an ill-fitting bra and jeans where the crotch has rubbed through, I can't help but think I am so lucky to be here. Firstly to have passed security. But, mainly, because this industry is tough. And to be on this lot, to be in this realm, even if it's for 10 mins: I'm really grateful.

I'm going in for my meeting now.

Also, if Oprah walks out of this building next to me I will pass away.

As you probably know, I've since left Canberra radio, and now present national weekend breakfast across the HIT network.

Yes. National. Six years ago, I set it as my goal and I bloody got there.

So, that's me. That's how I got here. That's why you're reading this book.

It's not the end, though. This is the beginning. That's why this isn't an autobiography.

---

* Spoiler alert: I did not see Oprah.

There have been so many times when I have wanted to give up. So many times. But I'm so glad I listened to the little voice inside of me that said, 'Don't give up, keep going.' I guess, on reflection, I'm so glad I got so many 'no's and 'unfortunately's, because of how appreciative I am of the 'yes's.

I am all too aware that I will continue to get 'no's and 'unfortunately's, and that's fine . . . because I'll just keep going and push through. I've done it before. I'm well versed.

Don't give up. Someone once told me that in a casting for a Telstra ad. She said: 'Outwork them, don't give up. Because your resilience will define your career.'

I'm glad I listened to her.

So now, you, reading this, listen to me.

Don't give up. Outwork them; your resilience will define your career.

It's strange how I tried to be an actor for so long, then realised the most successful role I would ever play would be myself.

A

A
IS FOR . . .

THE MOST AWKWARD THINGS IN LIFE

Is anyone else just really used to being awkward? I'm at a point where I'm like, *Oh, this is me now. This is who I am. I am just really awkward.* For a long time, I would get embarrassed. Now I think, *All in a day.*

Here's a brief list of awkward moments you might relate to (or not):

- Talking to someone you think is talking to you . . . but actually they're using handsfree.
- Pulling a door that says *Push*. Then trying to open the door again . . . by pulling. Not pushing.

- When the staff at the cinemas say, 'Enjoy the movie,' and you reply, 'Thanks, you too!'
- Thinking someone's going to high five you but they're just waving at someone behind you.
- Accidentally bitching about someone and not realising you're talking to that person's brother.
- Walking fast and accidentally getting to hold a stranger's hand. Also, swinging your arms when you walk and hitting someone's crotch.
- Saying goodbye to someone, then realising they're going the same way as you (the WORST).
- Going in for a hug and then realising, way too late, that the person just wanted a handshake.
- Asking someone at a store for clothing in a different size and realising they don't work there.
- Parallel parking in front of a café ('Look away, café patrons; why are you watching me? Go back to your phones.').
- When someone says they're going to a funeral and you say, without thinking, 'Have fun!'
- When you wave at someone you think you know and you *def* don't know them.
- Cuddling someone from behind and realising they're a stranger. (There is definitely a theme happening here.)
- Not checking your text messages before you send them. (Like the time I sent this gem to my boss: *Hey, I've sent you audio of my last wee. Enjoy.* He wrote back: *Tanya, I hope you meant week.* Luckily for him, I did. There was also that time I texted my mum telling her about the awesome clock shop I'd found:

Me: *Mum, I found an amazing cock shop. They have huge ones here. Just the kind you like. I'll take a pic for you, you'll love it!*

Mum: *That's good darling. I don't need to know about that though. Don't send pictures!*

Me: *I meant clock. Huge clocks!!!*

Mum: *I'm not judging, whatever you get up to is your business.*

Me: *I meant clock, Mum.*

Mum: *Don't send pictures Tanya.*

Me: *Mum, I meant clocks and we should come here together for a holiday.*

Mum: *It's OK darling, that's an alone activity.*

ADULT EXPECTATIONS

The way I thought I was going to be as an adult is significantly different from the way I actually am. Now I think my expectation just isn't living up to the reality . . .

Expectation: Married with kids. The kids are always dressed well and have nice manners.
Reality: Eating grated cheese. From the bag.

Expectation: Amazing family events and barbies.
Reality: Napping all day.

Expectation: Knowing how to do my tax and knowing how banking works.
Reality: Crying while googling 'how to live'.

Expectation: Always groomed and amazing.

Reality: *Ah, it will do. Ugg boots. Where is my bra? Fuck it, I'll go to Coles pantless and braless. I have no dignity or shame.*

Expectation: Huge seven-bedroom phenomenal house. The *Home Alone* house!

Reality: 'Yeah, hi, Ray White, there's another rat infestation in the flat, and the hole in the wall has gotten so bad, I can see the neighbours touching themselves.'

Expectation: More than enough money to live comfortably.

Reality: 'HEY, MUM! . . . Can I borrow $60? I will def pay you back.'

B

B

IS FOR...

BANK

I recently went to the bank to ask about a home loan.

I wore a blazer to an informal meeting, because I don't know how to live. I just thought: *Look important and fancy— like you know things. Wear a blazer.*

I now know the blazer was too much. The bank person I spoke to was in jeggings.

All I really wanted to know was how much I needed for a deposit, and stuff like that. Pretty basic. But when you go in, they have to go through all your banking history, to see if you're a good candidate for a loan.

The woman in jeggings looked me up and down as she went through my internet banking with me, asking me questions along the way.

'Right, Tanya,' she says. 'There's just a few more questions before we can proceed. I've noticed you've got some strange transactions going on here.'

'Oh,' I say, racking my brain. *What was the last thing you bought online, you idiot?* My brain is frazzled and can't keep up. Bank Lady keeps going, though.

'Who is . . . "Pimp Monies"?' she asks.

'Oh,' I say, trying not to laugh. 'Um . . .'

'And who is "Amy Is My Pimp"?'

I can't speak. I'm about to crack it.

She looks me square in the eye. 'Do you have . . . another source of income?'

I shake my head. 'No,' I say, relieved that this is her main concern. 'It's just a joke! I never have any cash on me, so I always transfer money to my friends to pay them back, and I think it's funny to write "pimp money" as the description. You know?'

She does not know.

'Okay,' she says. 'So, this isn't real? You're not . . . a "lady of the night"?'

'No!' I say. 'I'm a radio announcer!'

'Okay,' Bank Lady says. 'And your friend isn't a pimp?'

'Oh no,' I say. 'She is.'

BROTHER

I have a 24-year-old brother.

When I was 27, single and living at home with my parents, because I was super successful, he was 19. For eight months, we shared a wall. By that, I mean his room was next to mine.

I would often hear him in there late at night doing random activities. I can only assume he was knitting, with all the banging of his elbows against the shared wall. And he must have always been sick with a cold, because there were so many tissues in his bin.

He didn't seem to like me all that much. I didn't know if it was an age thing or what. But he was always mad at me.

I remember him saying one day, 'Why does it take Alanna [our sister] an hour to get ready when she goes out, and it only takes you 15 minutes?'

I replied, 'Well, that's because I refuse to straighten my hair, I refuse to wear false eyelashes, I refuse to spend an hour doing my make-up.'

He said, 'That's why men *refuse* to go near you.'

How could I be mad when he had such awesome burns? He's a boy genius, if anything.

BALI

Bali is not for me. Yes, the cocktails are $3, and the massages are heaven, but it's fucking hot. And not Australia hot. It's dripping-wet-within-five-seconds-of-leaving-the-hotel hot. And I'm an air-con, sit-down gal. I'm also chubby, so walking anywhere in Bali means that the thigh rash is real. Here is my guide to Bali for chubby girls. You're welcome:

- A lot of what you can buy will just be sunglasses. That's okay, they're, like, $5 each.
- You will turn pink.
- The clothing often says *One size fits all*, but it should read *One size does not fit Tanya and it's confronting in a change room.*
- Everyone is hot and topless in the day clubs, and it will make you acutely aware you chose the #nuglyf.
- Invest in a kaftan and/or muumuu. Very Homer Simpson chic.
- Underboob sweat is real and often visible.
- The flight there and back can be awkward, because you're too chubby for the Jetstar seats.
- Your spray tan—the only thing that makes you feel slightly thinner—will come off almost immediately. Pack a bottle of fake tan.
- Pack your medicated thigh-rash cream of choice.
- Invest in bike shorts to wear under your kaftan/muumuu.
- Get a driver for the day because walking is hell in general, let alone in the humidity of Bali.
- You will sweat a lot, and it'll feel like you've exercised and you're losing weight. You are not. It's just Bali.

THE BEST THINGS EVER

Okay. Right. So, I guess some people think the best things ever are, like, the birth of your first child. Or your wedding day. Or finally getting your dream job.

For me, that stuff is okay. I mean, I imagine that when I have a kid and get married, I'll be stoked. But I like to look at the everyday. The things that happen to make the normal just that bit better (because living is hard). Those bits. They're my favourites. Here's a short list:

- When people cancel on plans you really didn't want to follow through on.
- Finding money in the pocket of that Cotton On hoodie you haven't worn since high school. Yass! Twelve dollars!
- The first time you wear brand-new undies or socks (seriously, how good does it feel to wear a new pair of socks? Orgasmic!).
- When you get on a plane and no one sits next to you.
- When you're doing anything and no one sits next to you.
- Getting into a bed with fresh sheets on it.
- When you're meant to be taking a five-hour bus trip and it turns out someone can drive you to the door of where you're meant to go. (Can I get an 'amen' up in here for that one?)
- When you get really good quality chicken in your kebab. You know what I mean.
- When you get in a new shower (e.g. in a hotel) and it has *amazing* water pressure.

- When you're a size 14 and you manage to fit into a 10 or a S (look, obviously the sizes run big wherever you're shopping, but I'm going to take this a win).
- When you start a new job and you realise the biscuit jar is fully stocked with Arnott's Assorted Creams and *nobody has touched the Kingstons yet*.
- When you bust out a new sponge to wash your dishes.
- When you're sleeping in on a Sunday and you can hear rain. This. Is. ACTUAL. Heaven.
- The first time you shave your legs and pits and . . . other areas with a new razor (yes, I do realise a lot of these things are to do with new stuff, and, yes, that is a hint that I am super lazy and often leave it, like, a few years between purchases).
- When you have a party at your house, and before everyone leaves at 9 p.m., they help clean up, and leave their alcohol and food (you end up with so many miscellaneous bags of chips).
- When you go to the shop counter expecting to pay full price for a pair of pants and they're actually 50 per cent off.
- Chicken Twisties.

BUSY DAD

Do you have certain things you call your mum about and other things you call your dad about?

I do.

Dad calls are like, 'I think my car needs a new engine or something? There is an engine light flashing on my dash-board—what do I do?'

Or 'Can you help me put my IKEA table together?'

Or 'Where's Mum?'

But Mum calls are epic. I'll call that woman at any hour, any day about every and any issue: 'I'm scared about becoming a mother' or 'What do you think happens when you die?'

I mean, I'll call her to just talk about my feelings to kill a two-hour solo car ride. I tell her everything and I ask her everything, sometimes too much. The thing is, she is an amazing, compassionate listener and I just rely on her.

So, a few years ago Mum goes on a cruise with the girls from work. Can you imagine five over-50 librarians on a cruise around the Pacific Islands? They would have been living their best lives! At the cruise comedy show every night, calling all the people who work on the ship by their first names and getting photos with them. Doing the pre-organised group activities like bingo and trivia and 'How to make a swan out of a watermelon' class on the pina colada deck. Dressing up for the themed nights and Karen being so tipsy she breaks her feature acrylic nail falling down after one too many Sex on the Beaches.

I can't.

I digress.

Because Mum is on this Librarians Gone Wild cruise, I haven't wanted to bother her/there is no reception in the middle of the ocean (I tried 40 times) . . . I have to call Dad.

I really want you to understand my dad. He's old school. A busy man; a businessman. Addicted to work, and he works seven days a week. He is highly strung and drinks a lot of coffee—actually the two jobs he's had in my lifetime have been selling chocolate and coffee (and we wonder why I have addiction issues?).

He's blunt, and suffers no fools and no nonsense. I am all fool and all nonsense.

Turns out he had one piece of advice he used for everything. Rinse and repeat. 'Well . . . life's not fair, Tanya.'

'Dad, I have a $900 phone bill and it sucks!'

'Well . . . life's not fair, Tanya.'

'Someone hit my car! What do I do? My car is stuffed. It's gunna cost me so much time waiting for it to get fixed.'

'Well . . . life's not fair, Tanya.'

'I wanna buy a house but it's so intense. How do I even get a home loan? What do I pay a solicitor for? It's hard getting into the property market.'

'Well . . . life's not fair, Tanya.'

The other day I parked my car on his lawn instead of the designated cemented parking area.

Once he found out, he yelled, 'Tanya, you've ruined my lawn!'

Know what I said?

'Sorry Dad.'

Jokes; I obviously said: 'Life's not fair, Kevin.'

PS Once Mum came back from the cruise, she made all our napkins into the shape of swans for two years afterwards.

BODY

Am I the only one who hates getting dressed in the morning?

I hate it. I have hated it for years. I have recently gained a lot of weight, quite quickly, which has made me hate getting dressed even more.

Sometimes I've been late to work because I've had mini breakdowns over how nothing fits and how gross I look in tops that fitted 3 months ago.

Sometimes I avoid mirrors. Sometimes I've avoided them to the point that I've actually left the house with panda eyes, or something stuck in my hair, completely oblivious.

I feel so anxious writing about this. I feel like no matter what I say about my body, it's wrong. People get really mad at me when I talk about my body honestly. I hear a lot of: 'You have a million followers on Facebook, you have such a huge platform . . . and you want to waste it by being negative about the way you look?' Some people tell me to think about the young people who follow me and who might be influenced by my honesty. Some people tell me I should use my platform to talk about body love and positivity. I get all that. I really do.

But, the truth is, I can't be body confident and body positive if I don't feel that way.

Right now, I'm the biggest I have ever been, and all I feel is uncomfortable.

(I want to be clear, this isn't about anyone else but me. I'm not shaming anyone, I'm talking about feelings. Explicitly *my* feelings. This just how I feel. I'm going to be completely honest and it's not going to be positive. But maybe some of you can relate.)

I feel totally at odds with my body.

It's uncomfortable to sit on a plane, or in a seat at the theatre, or even just in a café. My butt and thighs spill over the sides of chairs, which is really frustrating and makes me sad. I sweat a lot. My boobs are heavier. My face is bloated. My clothes feel strange on me. My undies are tight.

I hate shopping. I'm at the point where I don't fit into the clothing at the shops I've always gone to. Even the big sizes don't fit. Telling the shop assistants that I don't fit into the size I thought (or hoped) I might be/used to be is painful and awkward, especially when there are no larger sizes.

I wear jumpers constantly. I'm wearing one right now. It's 30 degrees outside but what can I do? I hate my arms. I can't tell you the last time I waved or even put my hands in the air or even wore a sleeveless top or dress.

I don't own shorts, playsuits or skirts; I can't wear them. I can't wear summer dresses anymore because the chub rub is so bad, and when I wear longer dresses, I put on bike shorts underneath to protect my thighs from chafing together.

I want to live in pyjamas. That sounds like the set-up to a joke but it's not; when I'm wearing pyjamas is the only time I'm truly comfortable.

I'm not writing this to make you feel uncomfortable or sorry for me . . . or to make you feel like you need to DM and tell me about a great PT you know or give me info about the keto diet. I'm writing this because it's the truth. I would love to be the kind of person who embraces her body at any size but . . . I'm just not. Frankly, it's very frustrating—even more so because I know that I did it to myself.

I have abused my body with fast food, almost daily, for months. I have eaten take-away for lunch, and then binged on chocolate and biscuits all afternoon, then had pizza and soft drink for dinner . . . then eaten chocolate again.

I have a complicated relationship with food.

I use food as a comfort. When things are going well, I give myself food as a reward. But, conversely, when I'm feeling low, I punish myself with food too. I eat for all occasions. I eat when I'm stressed. When I'm happy. When I'm tired. When I'm sad.

I know I need to change my relationship with food, but it's much more difficult than I could ever have imagined.

The truth is, though, that even when I weighed 30 kilos less than I do now, I still hated my body. I couldn't tell you a time that I was truly happy with my body and loved it. I don't think I've ever looked in the mirror and thought, *Damn, you look good*. Isn't that depressing?

So, I know that, as well as changing my relationship with food, I need to change the way I think about my body.

My goal? Here it is.

I want to be able to read this back in a year and not recognise myself in these words 'cause I love and am wholly proud of my body.

I want to get to a place where I love . . . or at least like my body every day. I don't want my body to be in my mind so much of the time, taking up precious space.

The funny thing is, even though I'm the biggest I've ever been, I'm also the happiest. I'm creating, and I'm enjoying what I'm creating. My career is going well, and perhaps that is down to me celebrating my brain and not putting all my focus on my body.

Even though I don't love my body, I've never loved my mind more. I am so proud of myself and of my accomplishments. I've never really been able to say that before. I have more confidence in my creativity than I have ever had. I feel strong. I feel like where I am is exactly where I should be.

I'm attempting to love myself/my body more—but it is hard and I have to actively work at it every day.

So, that's me and my body: a bit fucked up, a bit of a mess—but, actually, I reckon the way I feel is (depressingly) common. I want to love my body and I'm working on it, and if you feel the way I do, I invite you to work on loving yours too. Because if I've learned one thing, it's that life is too short to waste not loving yourself.

And that's just the truth.

C

IS FOR . . .

 CASTINGS I HAVE BEEN TO

Please know that I have not made these up. These are literally the descriptions in the scripts of 'characters' I've auditioned for. I mean . . .

- French prostitute
- Busty wench
- Chubby best friend
- Weight loss company Before Girl
- Brunette Girl Two

- Girl with obvious double chin
- Generic prostitute
- Actor who is clearly not athletic
- An everywoman who doesn't stand out. Bland. Plain.
- Prostitute snorting cocaine off her hand while peeing in the street
- Drunk bridesmaid
- Prostitute with a heart of gold
- Brunette 20-something. Maybe has a fringe?
- Trashy young mum who is comfortable with her stomach out in a crop top
- Female: moderately attractive
- Female with stumpy, chubby fingers; youngish
- Rotund girl who doesn't fit in
- Girl who has slept around. Looks rough around the edges.
- Big-breasted woman. Should have soft boobs that move when she laughs.

COMPARED WITH ROLES I *ACTUALLY* GOT

A piece of trash

This was a role in a school play about two frogs who lived in a polluted pond. Other kids in my class were cast as mermaids, fish, or beautiful, brightly coloured coral, and I played a piece of trash. Mum had to put me in a garbage bag and staple empty

Twisties wrappers to me. I still remember her tears as she clacked the chip packets onto the bag. I think she was crying because, even at the age of five, I was believable as trash.

Hobo 3

This was in *Little Shop of Horrors* in high school. My role was to lie down, passed out and holding a bottle in a bag, for an hour. I was only in Year Nine, and this turned out to be somewhat prophetic—I'd go on to do just that at uni every single night.

Prostitute

Actually, 'prostitute' *and* 'busty prostitute' appear on my acting CV nine times. Seven of those nine jobs were unpaid. Yep . . .

COUGAR

So, the thing is, I'm not even sure if I *am* a cougar. I mean, I'm 32. My boyfriend is 25.

According to a very reliable source I met on Twitter, I'm not a cougar, I'm a cradle snatcher. Charming. According to my parents, our set-up is 'unusual' and, according to a friend of mine, it's creepy. But, according to my boyfriend, Tom, and me, it's just a relationship.

But the minute I mention that Tom is younger than me, I get ready for the judgemental expressions, raised eyebrows, and barrage of comments and questions that will follow. Everything from 'So, you're, like, a cougar, huh?' to 'Ohhhh . . . someone's got a toyboy!' to everyone's favourite, 'I could NEVER date someone younger than me.'

To be completely honest, before I met Tom, I might have been guilty of thinking and saying these things myself. But now that I'm older I know that our relationship is normal . . . except for some very particular quirks. Like:

- Your younger partner will usually have *way* more energy than you. I mean, I'm lazy anyway, but even if I had the energy of a normal person, I couldn't keep up with Tom. He's always ready to go; I'm always ready for a nana nap. Even when I've just woken up from a nana nap.

- When you really think about the age gap, you'll feel a bit weird. Like, when I was at uni, my boyfriend was in primary school. Mmm. When I was at the uni bar, he was having a Le Snak at little lunch. Can't think about that one for too long. Ouch.

- People constantly say to you, 'Age is just a number.'

- You disagree on unusual things, such as they like to party and you like to be in trackpants and without a bra on a Friday and Saturday night. You want to look at homewares but he wants to hang out in the toy section.

- You're constantly trying, in vain, to fight the aging process, because you're all too aware that eventually that age gap will become very physically apparent.

- People will assume, that you, the older woman, are maternal, or teach or mentor your 'cub'. Nah. For me personally, it feels as if my boyfriend is older and wiser than me.

- You don't share pop culture references. (It KILLS ME that he doesn't know who All Saints are.)
- On the plus side, your friends make fun jokes like 'When he goes to the hospital, do you take him to the kids' ward?', or (if you're going out to eat) 'Should I call ahead and see if they have colouring in?'
- You often fight because they think celebrating means clubbing and you think it means Woolworths mud cake and a fork.

Look, all jokes aside, being a cougar is *hard*—if only because you feel forced to defend your relationship constantly. (Also, I feel it bears mentioning that one of my friends is in her 20s and is dating a guy in his 40s and nobody ever questions their relationship. Huh.)

CEO

So. Did you ever have that thing where you can't access anything online at work? No emails, no Facebook, no news sites—nothing?

It's happening to me right now.

My internet account has been blocked, and I think I know why.

It's because I saw this meme. It's of Lauren Conrad (if you don't know her, she was on a reality TV show called *The Hills* and now she's just on Instagram), and some obnoxious male radio presenter is asking her what her favourite position is.

And, without *blinking*, she goes: 'CEO.'

What. A. Boss.

Some sleazy guy asks her a sleazy question and she just owns him. I was so inspired; what a legend. I wish I could think that quickly.

I thought, *I'm at work, I have a spare 10 minutes to waste before lunch.* (I mean, who works at work anyway?) I was curious to know what companies are headed up and/or owned by women. I typed 'Women on top' into Google, thinking it would give me women in CEO or other senior management positions.

I got a lot of images of women.

In a lot of positions.

And they were on top.

Just not at the top of a corporate ladder.

So, now I can't access the internet at work and am going to have to have an awkward chat with my boss . . . but I think my boyfriend is in for a treat next time I see him.

CREATIVE

There's not a lot that gets me really fired up and crazy passionate but this topic does, so fair warning. I'm hitting the keyboard so hard as I type because this infuriates me so much.

So, you've read the intro to this book. Besides working in a few restaurants, I've only ever really worked in the creative industries. Which means people constantly ask me to work for free or for a schnitzel (for seven hours of work).

Anyone who works in a 'creative job' gets this. Everyone from actors, artists, designers and make-up artists, to writers, cakemakers, filmmakers, television personalities, photographers, and everything and anything in between.

I assume that it's because we genuinely love what we do that people assume we will do it for free.

Yes, you have to start somewhere, and all of us—no matter what industry—at some point will have worked for free to get experience and to get our foot in the door. That's not what this is about.

The below phrases have all been said to me.

'Can you do this for me? It's great experience!'

I cannot pay my rent, phone bill and for my groceries with 'experience'. There comes a point where we have done enough gigs to get experience and need to start charging.

'If you do this one free, we may pay you next time.'

You wouldn't say that to an accountant. This makes me see red. Saying 'we MAY pay you' isn't okay.

'It's not paid, but it's brilliant exposure for you.' OR 'It's a great opportunity.'

Is stilt walking and doing face painting for five hours for free at a kid's party that's three hours away good exposure? Really!? You paid for the catering. Why aren't my skills and services similarly valued?

I was once asked to emcee a two-day event, for seven hours a day. 'What was the fee?' you ask? The answer: 'It's a great opportunity for you, Tanya.'

'I'll pay you in beer.' OR 'It's not paid, but we'll give you free drinks!' OR 'It's unpaid. But we'll feed you.'

A STEAK isn't currency. I once got asked to do a two-hour trivia gig—weekly. It was at a place an hour away from my house, and when I asked about the fee they were insulted, then wrote, *Tanya, our offer is one steak per week*.

So, for three hours of work, I get a $12 steak (cost price $6).

It's not even an award wage. If I was a waitress, you would have to pay me at least $21 an hour. But for some reason, if a person works in the arts, it's okay to ask them to work for free and seemingly it's okay to be mad at them for asking if there is a fee.

'It's good for your CV/folio.'

Is it?

'I'll write you a great reference.'

I cannot pay my car rego with your reference.

'You cost how much?! That's out of our budget. Can you recommend someone cheaper?'

I mean, *really*?

'I haven't spoken to you in months/years but now I recognise your talent—remember how we were best friends? Can you do me a favour?'
This. Happens. Weekly. To. Me. This one infuriates me no end.

Us creatives are sensitive, and we don't want to let people down. We love to help where and when we can, but we need to be remunerated. Most of the time, we would love to help you out, but we just can't survive on exposure or experience. We need cash moneys to live.

For me, please show the creatives of this world some love . . . and bloody pay them for using their talent.

CAREER

Have you ever done a job you have no idea how to do?

I have. Twice.

Well, actually, that's not really true: I've done jobs I didn't know how to do my entire career.

But the jobs I really, really didn't know how to do? Yeah, I had no fucking clue. Allow me to explain.

The job I never should have been hired for: wardrobe assistant
Picture this: the year was 2010 (at least, I think it was; I can never remember exactly, because I was drinking a lot back then. At any rate, it was *close* to 2010). I was living my dream . . . as a wardrobe assistant. And when I say, 'living my dream', I mean 'getting paid— barely'. But I digress.

I was completely and utterly wrong for this job.

First, I can't sew. Second, I have no interest in learning how to sew. I *do* like costumes, but I *do not* like cleaning and packing them away, which was the essence of the job. To get myself through it, I spent more time wearing the costumes than I did cleaning them. I also 'treated myself' to more toilet breaks than were strictly necessary, and 'phone time', which was, um, just me playing on my phone.

So, how on earth did I get hired for a job I had *zero* interest in and was not at all qualified to do? I'm so glad you asked.

I lied in the interview. Straight-up lied.

I lied about being able to sew but, more importantly, I lied about being able to drive a manual car, which was a big part of the job, as I would have to transport the costumes around the city. I had never—ever—driven a manual car, but I was desperate for cash, so I lied.

I figured I'd have at least a week to practise before they'd let me near the company car to drive round the Sydney CBD. I was wrong.

On day one—day bloody one!—I had to drive the *manual* company car from the Opera House down to the Opera Centre in Elizabeth Street, Surry Hills. In peak hour.

Jesus Christ.

So, I'm there at the Opera House, with this manual (did I mention it was manual?) Opera Australia car. On day one. I was sweating bullets. I needed this job so badly, and I was so close to fucking it up completely.

I literally had no idea what to do. I didn't even know how to get the car to move. *How do I even turn it on? It's so easy in an auto! Why the fuck isn't this an auto!?*

I turned the key in the ignition. Nothing. I looked around, trying to find a magic button or something else—*anything*—that would help me. Instead, I found three pedals. *Three pedals. What the fuck do you need three pedals for?!*

I decided to go for it. I put my foot on what I now know is the clutch. The car started. *Yes.*

By this point, I was swearing, crying, and trying to figure out what I would wear as the defendant in the court case I would inevitably be involved in as a result of driving this car. The car had started, yes, but I still didn't know how to get it to, you know, move. Which seemed like a really important part of driving.

I thought through my options. *Do I call the Opera Centre? Call my boss? Stage my own death?* I needed the job—badly—and, besides that, I didn't want to piss off the Opera Australia team because I also did a little acting work for them, which I didn't want to lose.

Shit.

My heart was racing and I wanted to throw up.

I put the car in neutral and—not knowing what else to do—thrust my body backwards and forwards against the seatbelt to get her to move.

It moved.

I am a genius.

I played with the three pedals for a while and, eventually, I got her moving. *Thank god.* I willed myself to calm down and kept thinking: *Okay. You've made it this far, Hennessy. Just keep doing what you're doing and you'll be at the Opera Centre in no time. Off you go. You've got this.*

So, I finally made it out of the carpark and bunny-hopped my way down the road in peak-hour traffic. *I look like an idiot but who cares? I'm doing it. I can't believe it.*

Then I saw a hill.

Shit.

Shit fuck shit.

I was really crying at that point. And I was *really* swearing. I still had no idea what to do. So, I gave holding the hand-brake a crack. Nothing. I tried again. Nope. By about the 25th attempt (not hyperbole), I figured it out and cleared the hill.

It was simultaneously the most embarrassing and exhilarating thing that had ever happened to me.

I kept going, thinking: *Right. If the traffic doesn't stop and there are no more hills, I'll be fine.* I was like Dory in *Finding Nemo*: *just keep driving, just keep driving.* Except, unlike Dory, I was dropping f-bombs every 10 seconds or so.

Finally, I could see the Opera Centre. YES! I was on Elizabeth Street and I indicated left to go into the carpark. I visualised the movie they would make about this moment— girl overcomes great odds to park car—and then I saw it.

Another fucking hill.

From the street, I could see I'd have to drive the car up a driveway that was pretty much at a 90-degree angle. With the Sydney traffic banking behind me before I turned in, other drivers beeping frantically at this idiot in front of them, and the growing, dreadful realisation of my sheer incompetence, I was just the teensiest bit stressed. And by 'teensiest bit stressed', I mean 'ready to stop the car, throw the keys away and have a good lie-down on the road'.

I just couldn't get it up (that's what she said; sorry, it was just too obvious).

I tried and I tried and I tried. Nothing. I was getting more and more frustrated.

At one point, I managed to get the car halfway up the driveway . . . only to have it roll backwards into another car. *Shit a goddamn brick.* Luckily, the driver wasn't fazed and simply kept driving. Maybe this was some sort of weird solidarity of manual drivers: you hit me, I turn a blind eye. Whatever.

At last, my knight in shining armour arrived. An Australia Post driver parked his van, got out and asked if I needed help. I played it cool, of course, saying something like, 'Oh, sure, if you have time; otherwise, I'll be fine,' while internally screaming *YESSSSSSSS!*

The man climbed into the car, and expertly pushed and pulled on the clutch and pedals as I watched helplessly, and, in about 10 seconds flat, he had the car up the driveway and parked perfectly. Like the angel he was, he just about vanished into thin air as soon as it was done. Sir, if you are reading: you saved my life that day. Not to mention the Opera Australia car.

To say I was relieved is a massive understatement. My shirt was soaked through with sweat, my nerves were completely shot and my stomach was about to eject the contents of my breakfast (half a sausage roll), but I'd done it. Sure, I hit a car.

And sure, I hadn't done it completely alone. But I'd done it, goddammit.

Then I looked up and saw a very disgruntled senior employee of Opera Australia staring at me, arms crossed.

Fuck fuck fuck.

I am done.

'What was that?' he said. 'Did someone who is *not* an Opera employee just park the car? That's not allowed. Our insurance doesn't cover that.'

I said nothing.

'What on earth is going on?' he asked. 'Did someone who's not an Opera employee park the car? What did I just see?'

Still nothing.

'Who *are* you?' he asked.

Finally, I worked up the nerve to tell him what had happened (I left out a lot of the *fucks*, though).

Strangely, the man didn't get me fired. But he did say that I needed driving lessons (*obviously*), so, during work hours (seriously), one of the other staffers taught me how to drive a manual car. I did my normal job, and she sat in the car with me and taught me to drive it . . . and then I was fine.

To sum up: I lied in a job interview, was not punished for said lie, and then got taught to do the thing I'd said I could do . . . while being paid for it.

Lesson learned, right?

Wrong.

The job I should never have agreed to: dresser

Picture this: it's 2011. I'm still poor, still trying to be an actor, and still failing to be an actor.

I got a call from my friend Lydia, who worked in musical theatre.

'I'm working on this musical,' said Lydia. 'And they need dressers. Want me to put your name down? It's $1200 a week, plus you get a $100 bonus every week if you work all eight shows.'

I thought for about half a second before I replied, 'Ah, yes, I want you to put my name down.'

'You've done this before, right?' said Lydia. Responsible, sensible Lydia.

'Yeah,' I said. 'Of course.'

Lies. All lies. Again.

But, in my defence, I needed the money. A lot.

I also figured it couldn't be that hard. *I mean, getting people dressed? I get myself dressed (basically) every morning! How hard can it be?*

And yes, that's what a dresser does: literally puts costumes on actors before and during performances of live theatre, including opera, ballet and musicals. They're particularly necessary for big-budget musicals, as there are so many costumes and quick costume changes. Not to mention the costumes are really fucking expensive, so care needs to be taken when performers are removing the clothes and putting them back on. Dressers are responsible for looking after everything the actors wear on stage—the undergarments, petticoats, hats, shoes, earrings, necklaces, stockings, you name it—except for the wigs (there are separate people who do this). Dressers sew and fix a lot of costumes too. After months and months of wear and tear, sequins and beads inevitably fall off, hems fall down and buttons start to pop.

Again, I did not know how to sew. I was not a particularly quick person, moving-wise. And I didn't even really know how to dress myself.

And yet: I got the job.

On day one, I turned up and realised I'd done it again: *I'm in the wrong job, and I'm going to hate it, and I might get fired.* All the other dressers were wearing black, and carrying little bum bags full of needles and thread and other sewing gear.

I was carrying . . . a foot-long sub.

I don't know how—honestly—but I managed to get through 10 months of shows (that's eight shows a week, BTW) without sewing a single thing. I got the actors dressed, and then basically charmed the heck out of them and otherwise stayed quiet, so that nobody would ask me to do a damn thing.

Lesson learned?

No. I'm sure you're catching on to the idea here. I don't learn.

CLICKBAIT

I hate clickbait.

You know what I mean. When you're trawling through your newsfeed and you see a headline for a story that looks cool and interesting, but when you click through, you realise the headline is a complete lie? That.

It really gets my goat.

Recently, I saw a bit of clickbait that really drew me in:
JESS MAUBOY CELEBRATES HER ROOTS

I clicked right away. *How exciting! She never talks about that kind of stuff. You go girl*, I thought. *Feminism. Yes.*

The page came up and . . . it was just Jess talking about Darwin.

Fucking clickbait.

D

IS FOR . . .

DUH, TANYA

Have you ever judged something solely by the packaging? I feel like I do, all the time.

Royal purple? Cadbury chocolate! Red? Coke!

Recently, I was at my family home and really craving something sweet. Couldn't see any royal purple or red packages, but I did find a green bag that looked suspiciously like it contained health food—*But maybe sweet healthy*, I thought.

Opening the bag, I expected some sort of apricot–coconut hybrid that would . . . not quite hit the spot, but it'd be sweet enough. You know? Without looking, I popped one of the things in the bag into my mouth. I bit into it, and spat it straight out.

Ugh. Worst health food ever.

Well. Actually, maybe that's not true. It probably is healthy—for who it's intended for.

Dogs.

It was small pieces of dried kangaroo . . . something. (I'd prefer not to think too deeply about what part of the kangaroo it actually was.) The kind of thing you give to dogs when they roll over or sit down or shake your hand.

Oh my god.

As I dropped the bag on the counter (obviously, I do not clean up after myself at my parents' house), I thought: *Wow. That's, like, the third time this year I've eaten dog food.*

DOUGHNUTS

Not to exaggerate, but I've discovered a shop that will change your life. It's a clothing store. You know the deal: really on-trend clothes, shoes, hats and bags—the works.

But inside the shop . . . is another shop. Another shop that sells *doughnuts*. HALLELUJAH!

And not selling, like, an assorted iced dozen from Coles. (No shade, though, because Coles iced doughnuts are iconic.) This shop sells designer doughnuts.

So, obviously, I must visit this mythical place, right?

I travel an hour and a half to get there. (I have travelled some crazy distances for food; this isn't even the longest.)

I walk in, and HALLELUJAH! I have arrived.

The sales assistant—who is the most effortlessly cool woman alive—approaches me. She's painfully attractive. I feel so gross just standing next to her. Straight out of a magazine, she has a teeny-tiny frame. She's got on a white top with a black slip over it, a flanno around her hips, and she's wearing a choker. She has grey hair in a messy bun with a bow in it, and wears Doc Martens. She is so cool. I want to be her. I feel so intimidated. I'm terrified of hot people. I think about leaving but she opens her mouth and says, 'Oh, hey. The doughnuts are on the next level.'

Ah, sorry? Whoa . . . maybe I'm here to buy clothes?

'Hey, babe, doughnuts next level.'

Why didn't she say, 'Hey, can I help you?'

She assumed I was there solely for the doughnuts.

What an assumption.

I mean, she was correct.

So, maybe it wasn't an assumption.

Just really good customer service.

I bought four doughnuts and shame-ate them all on the hour-and-a-half drive home.

DISNEY DETECTIVE

I don't know anything. I literally know nothing. Well . . . besides about musical theatre and Disney.

You name a Disney film, I can give you a fun fact about it, or sing every one of its songs. I've been to two Disneylands

(Orlando and Hong Kong), and cried the whole time. I'm such a Disney tragic that if it was socially acceptable, I would wear mouse ears at all times.

I think my obsession started with *The Little Mermaid*. I just loved the mermaids . . . and the singing . . . and the crab.

But I was more obsessed with the antihero—the sea witch, Ursula. She was the ultimate villain and I loved her. I remember thinking, *I want to be her.* The villains always interested me far more than the heroines. The villains had more spunk, more sass; they were funny and layered. Why would you want to be boring and pretty Ariel when you could be the epic Ursula? I was a weird kid, rooting for the evil witch. I didn't want her to die, mainly so she would have more screen time.

There were so many incredible Disney female villains when I was growing up. I would also obsess over Maleficent, the Queen of Hearts; the Wicked Stepmother in *Cinderella*; and Cruella De Vil.

I loved the male villains too. I mean . . . Hades in *Hercules* (praise hands emoji) is my fave, followed closely by Scar from *The Lion King*. Scar was so bitter, funny and riddled with issues. Not (to my mind) boring and squeaky clean, like Mufasa (in saying that, Mufasa's death still haunts me #spoileralert).

The thing I always found bizarre was that the hero, Mufasa, and the villain, Scar, are brothers, right? Mufasa is 'The Lion King' and Scar is not. Ouch. Already the makings of a great movie, but did you ever think it was weird that one brother has an amazing, strong name like Mufasa and the other just has a nickname?

My thoughts were that surely he'd gained the scar later in life, rather than being born with it. So, what was Scar's birth name? After googling it (I don't leave the house much, so am often googling things like 'what was Scar from The Lion King's birth name?' and 'what time is it?'), I found out his birth name was Taka.

Then I found out that in Swahili, Mufasa means 'king' and Taka means 'trash'.

Seriously, that's weird parenting—it's like calling your kids 'Doctor' and 'Drug Dealer'.

But it's even more strange that the names the parents in *The Lion King* gave their kids were prophetic. Mufasa was the king, and Scar was kinda trashy.

Which has given me a great idea. I will be naming my kids 'Massage Therapist', 'Doughnut Maker' and 'Billionaire Who Gives Their Mum All Their Money'. It's a mouthful but I gotta take the chance. *The Lion King* told me to.

DUID (DRIVING UNDER THE INFLUENCE OF DISNEY)

So . . . I have some advice for you: if you're ever on a road trip, don't drive with the windows down. Use dat air-con, gurrrl.

Here's why.

One time, I was driving around with my cousin. Normally, I'd listen to the radio while driving, but we (mainly me) decided we would have a Disney singalong . . . which is NEVER a good idea when you aren't nine years old.

So, here we are driving around Toowoomba and we stop at a set of lights. I'm belting out a mean 'Colors of the Wind' from *Pocahontas*. Like, NAILING it.

I look to my left, mid punch to the sky (it's a very emotional part of the song), and, lo and behold, the hottest guy ever is sitting in the driver's seat of the car next to us, his arm casually hanging out the window, and happily watching the show I'm putting on.

Bloody hell. How embarrassing! I'm 29. And single . . . and he is HOT.

As soon as we make eye contact, I attempt to change the music, and, in my haste, accidently turn it up and skip to a track from the *High School Musical 2* soundtrack. At this point, I'm yelling at my cousin to turn the music off, because it's offensively LOUD—and just plain offensive, as it's from *High School Musical 2*—and because I can't figure out how to turn the volume down on her CD player. I'm desperate!

'TURN IT OFF. THERE IS THE HOTTEST GUY IN THAT CAR OVER THERE . . . TURN IT OFF!'

The music's turned off. Silence.

But I'm still flustered and yell, 'THIS GUY COULD BE THE LOVE OF . . . my . . . life . . .'

And it is around this point that I realise the window is down, and so old mate—aka hottest man alive—heard all of this. Yep, not only has he heard me call him the hottest guy alive, but he's also heard me say he could be the love of my life.

I am, obviously, mortified.

Silence ensues.

He opens his mouth and says . . . 'I always thought the first *High School Musical* was the best. Don't you think it was way better before it had a budget?'

Oh. My. God.

This IS the love of my life. He knows Disney . . . he knows High School Musical!

And before I get the chance to say anything back, the damn lights change and we're turning and he's going straight. Though, seeing that his numberplate says *Prince5s*, I don't think he is.

DAMAGES

I have never been sued. Surprised? Me too.

I've also never sued anyone but, given the chance (i.e. if I'd known about the concept), I probably would have sued my best friend in Year Three for stealing my idea of putting a sausage roll in a bread roll. Ash-LEY, if you're reading, you know the truth: it was *my* idea. We haven't spoken since. Mature, I know.

But we do live in a culture that will sue over anything and everything.

This Red Bull didn't give me literal wings . . . Sue.

I fell over in a public park . . . Sue.

My name is Sue . . . Sue.

I recently read that a Latin American author named Isabella Tanikumi wanted to sue Disney for plagiarism . . . for $250 million. She reckons the plot of *Frozen* is based on her 2010 autobiography, and not on Hans Christian Andersen's fairytale 'The Snow Queen'.

Is she for real?? Her AUTOBIOGRAPHY!

Just so we're all on the same page here, the dictionary defines an autobiography as *a written account of the life of a person written by that person.*

So, Isabella is saying that *Frozen*—the animated Disney film with a talking, walking, singing snowman and a princess who can turn anything into ice—is a written account of her life?

For those who don't know, *Frozen* is the story of two sisters, one of whom is magic. And not like magician-at-an-RSL magic, she's create-ice-from-nothing magic. (My eyebrows are raised, Isabella . . . can you do this? I assume you can, as this is the main plotline of *Frozen*.)

Magic Sister accidentally hurts Normal Sister with her ice magic (i.e., her ability to shoot ice from her hands, not to be confused with the ice-cream topping). The family takes the injured sister to a family of trolls, who are rocks until they're awakened. The troll king saves the sister's life and tells the magic sister to stop being magic. Still with us, Issy?

Then the sisters' parents die and Magic Sister becomes queen. She loses it during the coronation (big events are stressful, I get it) and the whole town witnesses her doing her ice magic (again, not the topping), so she runs away, accidentally freezing the entire town along the way.

Then she sings a song and transforms into a more sequined-cape-wearing sort of queen who creates an entire mansion OUT OF ICE . . . FROM. HER. HANDS! (Isabella, do you do this on a sneaky weekend away with the girls when you can't afford a hotel?)

Meanwhile, Normal Sister has met a sassy singing snowman. Yes. A singing snowman. I assume Isabella also had a snowman friend.

Blah blah blah—more songs, more trolls, more choreographed dancing, a few more ice disasters.

Finally, Normal Sister is on the brink of death (sorry, spoiler alert) and Magic Sister saves her in the nick of time. This also has the fortunate effect of breaking the spell on the frozen town and melting all the ice as the sun comes out. You would think that the sassy snowman would melt. But he doesn't. That's confusing. (But because it's Isabella's life story, I'm sure she can explain that.)

That's it.

Now, Isabella, I don't know you, and you very well could have ice-magic powers—but I honestly doubt it. I don't want to be a hater, but I just really don't think your life story has been stolen by Disney's *Frozen*, seeing as though you cannot prove that you have ice-magic powers, and nor can you prove the existence of a sassy snowman *or* a troll king.

Isabella, I have three words for you, babes . . .

Let it go (copyright Disney 2013).

E

E
IS FOR...

EXERCISE

Ha nah, there is literally nothing in here because exercise is the worst.

Seriously, there is nothing.

Literally nothing.

You can use these pages to doodle.

You still secretly think I'm gunna write something, don't you?

Nope.

How good is bread?

F

IS FOR...

FANCY

I went out to dinner with some friends the other night. They picked the place. It was this fancy Italian restaurant. Beautiful. You know the kind of place, with really full-on mood lighting— it's always too dark—obnoxiously large wine glasses, and classical music being played.

Anyway.

I didn't really realise it would be super fancy, and I rocked up in my normal look: no make-up, messy bun, dirty thongs, and jeans with a ripped crotch. In my defence: I'd just come from work.

I was with two friends, who wore linen, and clothes they'd ironed. (I don't own an iron.) They smelled like the Myer perfume area and just looked expensive. I looked like their sponsor child.

I honestly don't get how some people just look expensive. I know you know what I'm talking about. They are the kind of people who can wear Best & Less and make it look like Prada. I don't get it. I can't look expensive. I just can't. Honestly, even if I wore Dior, I'd manage to make it look like it was from the sale rack at Cotton On.

Either way, I was a fish out of water. I don't know how, or why, the staff even let me in, with the way I was dressed.

I seriously don't like fancy places. At all. I find them wanky and fake, and they make me feel uncomfortable. I think even if I was super rich, I wouldn't like them. It's the pretentiousness of it all. These environments seem so false.

But I sat down anyway, and the waitress put a white napkin on my lap. The boys ordered a carafe and some antipasti. I didn't know what either of those things were but I nodded along and generally made affirmative noises because I didn't want them to realise I had no idea what they were talking about.

I hadn't yet looked at the menu but, because the place was so fancy, my only thought was *How much is this going to cost me?*

Then another waiter came over to tell us the specials . . . in Italian. The boys were nodding along as if this foreign language made sense to them, and I was like . . . *Um. What? Come again?*

In the end, I looked at the physical menu but, of course, that was written in Italian too. *Fuck me dead.* Prosciutto San Daniele, rucola and reggiano pizza—*What is that?* I didn't want to give away that I didn't know. I was so stressed.

When the waitress came back, I just pointed at the menu and said, 'This.' I got a surprise gnocchi, which was—to its credit—unbelievable.

When I'm confronted with situations like these, instead of retreating into myself or drinking through them, like a normal person, I tend to overcompensate. So, I pretended I was as fancy as my surroundings by talking in a weird fake British accent, and I even put on my reading glasses, to make me look like a creative, rich 'This is my messy aesthetic' type. But I think I blew it when we paid the bill.

'I love your top,' the waitress said as she took my credit card.

'Thanks!' I said. I also loved my top. 'I got it at Supré, like, four years ago,' I went on, not seeing the look on her face. 'It was $15 but, actually, they reduced it because it has a rip in the back, see?' I turned around so she could see the small tear near my bra strap. 'Also, can I pay with half cash, half card? Also, if there's no money on the card, I might have to dance to pay the bill.'

Oh, how I laughed.

The waitress stared at me and just nodded, taking my credit card and numbly passing it through the scanner. Tough crowd.

Truth be told, I'm more of a Domino's girl. I know that now.

Domino's is Italian food that you can order to be taken to your house, and that you can eat lying down in your pyjamas.

You can also get chicken wings, Sprite and chocolate mousse for $28. I'm always going to be more comfortable in a place of bralessness and mousse.

Domino's girl for lyf.

FAKE . . . TAN

I'm a better person when I'm tanned. Fake tanned, obvs. Because being outside in the sun is not for me. I don't know how some people can just lie in the sun, tanning, for six hours a day. So boring.

I'm a weekly fake tanner. Well, I try. Consistency has never been my strong suit.

But once I'm freshly (fake) tanned, I become someone else. It's as though the tan awakens something in me. I'm like a caterpillar coming out of a cocoon . . . and I become a super-arrogant butterfly.

I think I look amazing tanned. In my mind, I am better than everyone, because *tanned*. Get out of my way, peasants, I am superior. I am tanned.

Seriously, fake tan gives me so much confidence (vodka does the same thing).

I'm sure you can relate.

Before Tanning: Walking down the street awkwardly, not wanting anyone to look at you.

After Tanning: Strutting in slow motion, while Fergie's 'Glamorous' plays.

Before Tanning: 'Nah, I won't go out tonight. I feel gross;
I don't want anyone to look at me; I'm fat.'
After Tanning: 'I will go out. I'll go nude. I am heaven. I am
a god. No, I am better than a god. I want everyone to
see me. Let's FaceTime all my exes.'

Before Tanning: 'No, I don't wanna be in the group photo.'
After Tanning: 'Everyone, get out of the way. I AM the
photo.'

FIRST KID VS LAST KID

It's always so interesting when your friends have kids and
you're still having trouble figuring out how to sell your car:
'Dad, can you sell this for me?'

Some of my friends have three kids apiece, and it's also so
interesting to see the way they are with their last one versus
how they were with the first one.

First: All her toys are bespoke and brand new.
Last: Her toys are taken from doctors' surgeries and old
Happy Meals.

First: Her food is all handmade, by me, and is all organic,
with heaps of veggies.
Last: She can have KFC at six weeks, right?

First: I got this $4500 bassinet.
Last: I think she'll be fine in a shoebox . . . we'll put a
pillow in it.

First: Her pram was $7K and I love it.

Last: I found this pram in an alley where a homeless man was playing with himself.

First: I love her so much.

Last: I think her name is Ruby; I'm literally not sure . . . it could be Rose.

(To reiterate, this is a joke and not to be taken seriously! No one I know has put their kid in a shoebox! It was a spare drawer.)

FRIENDS

My friend Tom is an idiot.

The best kind of idiot.

The kind who says you can't stay at his house even though he has a spare room, because that's the gift-wrapping room and you can't possibly stay in there.

The kind who knows all the choreography from every Britney Spears film clip but can't find his tax file number.

The kind who sends you a card that reads *You're beautiful without make-up* but when you open it up, you see that he's written *JOKES* on the inside.

The kind who has rhinestone glasses, laptop and phone case . . . because so does Rihanna.

The kind who vacuums in pole-dancing heels and sequined shorts because he won Mr Winter Wonderland 2011 for pole dancing (and won't shut up about it).

The kind who calls you 45 times and when you don't pick up, texts you that it's *urgent* and that it's *an emergency.* You quickly call him back, thinking he's been in a car accident or his mother has died . . . but his emergency is that he's at a Spotlight sale and doesn't know if he should get pink leopard-print or faux-fur throw pillows for his bed.

He is a stone-cold weirdo. Flamboyant, fierce and fabulous. I love him.

Tom and I worked together for a while, and it was so much fun. We would skive off together, and muck around and generally create havoc.

But for a few weeks in 2013, something really strange happened to Tom.

It started when he came into work with scratches all over him. On his face, wrists, neck and arms. Odd, thin scratches.

Tom didn't know what was happening, didn't know how he kept getting these scratches. It was so weird. I'd just seen the movie *Stigmata*, so, obviously, I figured he was being scratched from the inside by the Antichrist.

Where were these mystery scratches coming from? Tom and I went through his daily routines. Was he walking past a bush every day? Had he adopted a cat he'd forgotten about? What was he coming into contact with that was causing these random scratches?

After a few weeks, it was genuinely scaring us. I wanted Tom to go and see a doctor because neither of us could figure it out.

Then, one day, Tom comes in and confidently proclaims, 'Oh my god! I know what it is! It's my sequins! My sequined Kylie Minogue pillow-and-doona set! The sequins are scratching me!'

Obviously, I should have suggested this on day one.

A few weeks later, I noticed that Tom *still* had scratches on his arms.

'What's going on?' I said. 'Didn't you figure out it was the pillows?'

'Yeah,' he said. 'The Kylie Minogue pillow-and-doona set.'

'Right,' I said. 'So, you got rid of them?'

He looked at me like I had two heads. 'Get rid of them? Why would I do that?'

Told you.

He's an idiot.

But the best kind.

FACEBOOK

I used to love Facebook. Not anymore. It's become passive aggressive, rude, and it's hurting my damn feelings. Facebook has become a bitchy high school girl.

I'm not talking about the people on it or even in the stories in my newsfeed. I mean actual Facebook. Well . . . the advertising, anyway. Those ads on the right-hand side of the page or the ones that are integrated into your feeds. The recommended, sponsored and suggested pages are what I'm talking about. To be honest, I feel like they are trying to tell me something, and what they are trying to tell me . . . it isn't great.

The thing is, I know that these ads are targeted. They're sent to you based on stuff you google, the age you say you are on Facebook, where you live, even the pics you upload and your statuses.

But sometimes these ads are confronting, and do nothing more than remind you how sad your life can be.

Here are the last few weeks in my feed:

Stylists in your area now

Cover those greys.

Finally, a way to lose your double chin!

Feeling old? Considered botox?

Lady moustache? We can fix that!

Over 30 and not married? Ways to get him to pop the question

Oreo Cadbury chocolate now available in a Coles near you

24-hour McDonald's breakfast in your area (In saying that, I did follow up on this.)

Seriously. Facebook ads are suggesting (correctly, which is even sadder) that I make poor fashion choices, I'm going grey, I have a double chin, I need botox, I have a moustache, I'm desperate to be married, I enjoy the combination of Oreo and chocolate (what human doesn't?) and I love McDonald's. I mean, many of these are true. And yes, I clicked on all of them. But, man, it hurts. It's like my sad life is being reflected back at me.

This isn't even the first time Facebook has come at me with its passive-aggressive life suggestions. When I broke up with my boyfriend seven years ago, I got this:

Feeling flirty?

Find singles in your area. Gorgeous guys want to meet YOU!

Go on a date tonight!

Fine. But a year later, it was clear Facebook had given up on me. Here's what I was getting 12 months down the track:

Buy Dine for your feline

Get into the gym and lose a dress size

Speed dating: get back on the horse!

After three years without a dude in any of my pics, this is what Facebook served me up:

Want to get your ex back? Here's how

Ashley Madison: meet a married man today

So you're thinking of freezing your eggs

Just before I met my current boyfriend, I got:

Find your lesbian match at eHarmony.com

I guess it's not all bad. I did meet a lovely lady named Melissa.

PS Don't even get me started on Facebook memories or, as I like to call it, 'photos of you when you were thinner and hotter'.

(NEW) FRIENDS

How weird is the way you act around your old friends compared with how you act around your new friends? And it's not until you're with your old friends that you realise there's a distinct difference. For example:

New friend: Oh my god, I love your top!
Old friend: You look gross in that top. Actually, I've never seen you look so bad.

New friend: Should we get two dishes and share?
Old friend: I'm getting my meal and you get your own, and if you steal one single chip, I will stick a fork in your hand. If you want chips, order chips.

New friend: Hey, babe. (*Followed by affectionate kisses and hugs.*)
Old friend: I have my period. Don't touch me.

New friend: Hey! Wanna come over for movies and popcorn?
Old friend: You can come over if you really want, but I have things to do, so don't make eye contact or talk to me.

New friend: Tell me about your parents. What are their middle names? Is your mum's middle name your great-grandmother's name? Oh my god, how interesting.

Old friend: *Nothing. Just sitting together, not talking, both on separate phones, for three hours.*

New friend: Let's take a pic—duck face!

Old friends: I don't need any more pics of you on my Insta. It'll give people the impression we spend too much time together. Also, where's my *Grease 2* DVD? I need my fucking top back too. I hope you didn't stretch it out with your massive boobs.

G IS FOR...

GYM

Does anyone else procrastinate about exercise to the extreme? Like, when you know you need to go for a walk—not even so much for the physical benefits but just to clear your head—and even the thought of doing it makes you want to poke yourself in the eye repeatedly? So, you put it off and put it off because your motivation is minus a thousand.

That's me every day.

Here are some of the excuses I've used to get out of exercise:

- It's too hot today.
- It's too cold today.
- It may rain today.

- I don't want to get sunburned.
- My feet hurt.
- I'm too tired.
- My iPhone isn't charged.
- I can't find my headphones.
- I have a migraine.
- I'm bloated.
- I can't find my shoes.
- I can't find my bra.
- I'll definitely exercise more when I get new gym gear.
- This new gym gear is a bit tight. I'll exercise more when I've lost a bit of weight and fit into it better.

I'm honestly at a point of such low motivation that if someone said, 'Tanya, you will die if you don't exercise today,' I'd be like, 'Well, I've had a pretty good run.'

THINGS I THINK ABOUT AT THE GYM

- *Why am I here?*
- *I hate it here.*
- *Everyone knows I don't belong here.*
- *Is this the highest the air-con goes?*
- *Is there an exercise I can do where I don't sweat?*
- *Have I been on this treadmill long enough that the chick next to me won't judge me when I leave?*

- I am very pink right now.
- How does everyone else know how to use this equipment?! Who taught them?
- Remember not to do any exercises that show the hole in your crotch from your chub-rub friction.
- I hope I cut the Kmart tag off my top, so everyone thinks it's really Lorna Jane.
- I regret every takeaway meal I have ever had.
- How long do I rest in between sets? Like, seven to nine months?
- Why does that girl look so good? Oh . . . because she's here all the time. Yep. Right.

GLAMOUR

What's the deal with kids looking super mature these days?

They are so well put together, I can't even tell how old they are.

I remember being 14, and that was not what I was like. I was *not* glamorous, wearing cool clothes, with contour, to school. At 14, I was at an all-time low when it came to appearances. I dyed my dark brown hair blond with Napro Country Colours. Instead of coming out an alluring shade of golden–beige, it came out . . . a solid shade of orange. You know the tone. It's rough on the eyes.

On top of that, I decided to cut my hair really short, for reasons currently unknown to me. So, I had maybe five centimetres of hair, and butterfly clips covering any spare surface. Horrific.

(Sadly, I can't share any photos of myself at this time because I refused to have any taken.)

For some reason, I was living in beige Billabong corduroy pants and various other surf-brand T-shirts. Oh, and for some reason, it was really cool to wear kids' backpacks when I was at school, so I was rocking around with a Barbie bag.

We never wore designer stuff, like kids do now. I saw a 15-year-old with a Gucci belt the other day. Shit. (NB: she may have been 40; I have bad eyesight.)

Again, when I was growing up, it was all about surf brands. I HAD to wear Rusty, Billabong, Quiksilver, Roxy and, at a pinch, Bad Girl. Despite the fact I was more of a 'write a poem in a dark corner' kid than a surfy bikini-wearing kid, there was no choice: I needed to be wearing surf brands.

It's weird that when you're a teen, you never want to be different, so you demand that your parents buy you the same $150 Vans shoes your mates have. You desperately need that $90 pink Roxy jumper and the $45 wetsuit-style Billabong pencil case.

Then it all changes: the adult me will never buy expensive clothes. In fact, I gloat about my ability to be mega povo. 'Check out my thongs! I got them for $2 from Big W!' But when I was at high school, I would rather have died than worn anything from the brand Mango.

By the way, the following moment really sums up my teenage years.

I wrote a letter to a boy I liked, asking him if he wanted to go out with me, and gave it to him at recess. It said this:

Will you go out with me?
Yes
No
Maybe
(Please circle)

I am not kidding.

The boy gave it back to me in art class. I was so excited to see what he'd circled.

Oh my god. What did he circle? Oh My God. HE WROTE BACK!!! I opened the note.

Not *yes*.

Not *no*.

Not *maybe*.

He'd drawn another box, next to which he'd written *fuck no*. Then he circled that box.

Thank you, sir.

My 14-year-old self is so jealous of the glamour and finesse of teenagers nowadays. But my 32-year-old self is glad I've had my horrendous teenage experiences, because now I know never, ever to dye my hair from a box, just because the model on it looks hot. I'm glad I learned that lesson then—not now.

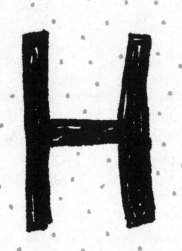

H
IS FOR...

HOLIDAYS

Every year we sing 'The Twelve Days of Christmas' (don't we?!)—but do we ever actually stop to think about the lyrics?

Nope.

I hadn't. Until this year.

So, as I see it, this is a love song, right? Presumably, this man is buying his true love an abundance of gifts—and I mean the least practical, crappiest gifts ever.

Come on. *This* is the stuff he gives to his true love?

A partridge in a pear tree: Okay. A bird and some fruit. Instagrammable. Solid gift. Ten points.

Two turtle doves: Mate, how many birds does one chick need? But sure. Three birds is manageable.

Three French hens: That's six birds now. Unnecessary. Also: messy.

Four calling birds: Annnnnddddd that's now 10 birds. These ones are calling—that's gunna be loud and annoying.

Five gold rings: None of which are engagement rings, which is probably what she ACTUALLY wants. More to the point, are these legit gold rings or Lovisa gold rings that turn your fingers green? Because that should be specified in the song.

Six geese a-laying: Current bird total—16.

Seven swans a-swimming: What is with this guy and birds?!

Eight maids a-milking: Very hard to regift.

Nine ladies dancing: Who is this guy? What man in his right mind would buy a woman *nine ladies dancing*? That's definitely a gift for him. Definitely.

Ten lords a-leaping: Just get her a Sportsgirl voucher, bro.

Eleven pipers piping: Remember when you learned to play the recorder in school? And everyone played together, but kind of at different times? It was agony. That's how I imagine this gift.

Twelve drummers drumming: Okay, now it is clear he's taking the piss. Who the hell wants one drummer, let alone 12 of them?

Have I overthought this!? Yes. OBVIOUSLY. But the real question is: how come nobody ever wondered why this dude got this chick *23 birds* for Christmas?

I mean, that is some serious serial-killer shit right there.

IF I WROTE A CHRISTMAS ALBUM . . .

You name a celebrity and they have a Christmas album . . . Sia, Hanson, Gwen Stefani and Blake Shelton all have Christmas albums. The songs include 'You Make It Feel Like Christmas', 'My Gift Is You' and 'Under the Christmas Lights'. Same boring, romanticised crap. Even the older stuff:

- 'I Saw Mommy Kissing Santa Claus'? A Christmas song about adultery.
- 'Santa Baby'? Sexual Christmas song. Ew.
- 'White Christmas'? Racist.

What I'm looking for is a more realistic Christmas album. I have the titles; I just need a songwriter. Here is the proposed tracklist:

- 'Christmas Is a Hard Time of Year (Because My Family Hate Each Other)'
- 'Jesus (Is Santa's Work Friend)'
- 'Santa Photos Are Overpriced' (featuring Samantha Jade)
- 'Christmas Decorations Don't Need to be up in October'
- 'That Christmas Sweater Isn't Necessary in Australia'
- 'You Have Clearly Regifted This' (featuring Justice Crew)
- 'All I Want for Christmas Is a Bunnings Voucher'
- 'I've Eaten All the Cadbury Chocolate-covered Peanuts We Bought for Christmas and it's November'

- 'Another Scented Candle'
- 'I Can't Wrap Circular Objects'

Hands up if you're not a fan of New Year's Eve! You can't see me right now (or can you?) but my hand is up.

I do not like New Year's Eve. Nope. Never have.

I just don't get the hype. I have never organised an event or prearranged anything for New Year's in my life (I sound fun, right?). Never. As a result, I always end up working (fine by me) or, failing that, I'll rock up to a friend's neighbourhood barbecue at the last minute. If I'm particularly desperate, I'll watch the fireworks on TV with my parents (just a quick sidenote: that is both the saddest and truest statement I have ever written).

Anyway, I just don't get the thing about New Year's Eve. It seems like so much fanfare for one night. Yes, we are ringing in the new year, and for some people that's important, but it just isn't for me. The pressure to do something amazing is so full on. I stay off social media on NYE because all I do is compare my thing to others and I feel like I'm failing. But I know I'm not. Because this is a choice. I just don't really rate New Year's. Easter . . . that's a different story, because Cadbury.

I don't get the fuss about New Year's resolutions either. The way I see it, people set themselves these crazy goals . . . and inevitably get depressed after about a month because they can't stick to them.

I feel like resolutions would be better—easier to stick to, that is, and more achievable—if we made them more realistic.

Like, if your resolution is to buy a house, quit smoking, lose 35 kilos, get that promotion and go holidaying in Europe, it's not going to happen. Let's just be upfront about that.

Aim realistically, people. Make your New Year's resolution *achievable*. Like 'I resolve to watch several TV series in one sitting.' Or 'This year, I'm going to eat more ice-cream.' Or maybe 'The year 2018 is the year I complain more.' Stuff like that. Boom. You could nail them by New Year's Day. You're welcome.

HOUSEMATES

Living with people is hard. I've done it all when it comes to accommodation . . . everything from a uni dorm room with 25 people to living solo.

The worst housemate I ever had was one who played the bagpipes. Do you know how loud bagpipes are? Shiiiiit.

I've never wanted to kill a man more.

One of my most memorable housemates was called Phoebe. She was everything I wasn't. Organised, tall and blond.

I was 19 and she was 21. For a uni student, man, did she have her shit together. She was an event manager/producer and just lived for organising things. Her love for an Excel spreadsheet was real. I really looked up to her and respected her. She was something of a den mother to me. Loving, but firm when she needed to be, because I was a bit wild at uni.

Phoebe was the kinda gal who always embraced my quirks. I remember this one themed uni bar night—the theme was

'Back to School'. Everyone came over for pre-drinks at ours and, of course, all the girls wore short school dresses with white pull-up socks, Britney Spears, 'Baby One More Time' style. Schoolgirl but, like, slutty. Which makes so much sense.

I guess I missed the sexy-schoolgirl memo. Because I dressed as a private-school boy. I named myself Graham and spoke with a lisp.

I bought high-waisted shorts and a button-up shirt, and a backflap hat (with an asthma puffer in it).

I thought it was supposed to be more like 'funny dress-up' not 'sexy dress-up'. I was 19. It is clear to me now why I didn't have a boyfriend at uni. I feel like this story says a lot about me as a person. Phoebe never judged me, though.

Phoebe was the kinda gal who would, if I had no petrol, because I had no money to buy it, always drive me to rehearsals. I mean, she would be mad at me for not 'budgeting correctly' but I knew the anger came from a good place. Phoebe was the kinda gal who was always patient. One day when I was really sunburned and really tired, I grabbed a white tube from the bathroom, thinking it was aloe vera. After 30 seconds, I realised it was actually Deep Heat. She was there for me through the tears.

Because she was older and wiser, she used to do the grocery shopping, and I would just kick in half the cost. This worked really well for me because she would cook for us too. At uni I was a loose cannon, so if she hadn't cooked, I wouldn't have eaten. (I had more Green Apple UDL in my blood than I had blood.)

As we shared the grocery bills, we were each entitled to half the groceries. Which meant half of all the healthy food was mine. Ugh, but this also meant half of all the naughty food was mine. *Yassss!* Namely, half the Mint Slices were mine. I think I wore Phoebe's patience pretty thin the week I opened the Mint Slice packet and there were only two left in the tray, and in front of the biscuits was a note.

It read, *Tanya, don't you think you've had enough?*

I clearly hadn't, because I ate those last two Mint Slices.
That was the first time Phoebe ever really got mad at me.
I understood that, though.
You should never fuck with someone's Mint Slices.

I

IS FOR . . .

IMPULSE

Do you ever get really excited at the Easter show, or even at a market, and buy stupid things? You get so into it all, you go wild and spend! You know what I mean. You're at a country fair and they're selling arseless chaps, and you think: *I do really need these. I need to buy them despite the fact I've never thought of buying them ever before, and they're $700.* You get swept up in the moment. Well . . . I do. The worst thing is, I justify every stupid purchase and so I never, ever learn from them.

Here are some stupid things I've bought at markets or fairs:

- An Akubra for $250 at a rodeo. (Why was I even at a rodeo?) Everyone else was wearing them and I got confused. I justified it with: 'Well, everyone needs a hat and I don't own one. This is a good investment.' The thing is, I almost never go outside. I have no need for a hat, let alone a $250 Akubra!

- A whip. I bought a fucking whip, again at a country-fair-type thing. It was $100. I've never used it. WHY DID WHOEVER I WAS WITH LET ME BUY IT?!

- I bought a motorbike jacket when I was at a market in Sydney. Like, for riding actual motorbikes. I don't even own a motorbike! I justified it with: 'Oh, I'll wear this heaps; it's real leather.' I didn't wear it heaps. I did, however, for years wear a Jay Jays pleather jacket I found on a bus. Figure that one out.

- A clock made out of a flattened Coke bottle. I don't even like Coke and I can't read analogue clocks! It was $60! I want to slap myself.

- Pet rocks. Like, a rock, with googly eyes from Spotlight hot glued on, and spray-painted by an eccentric woman in her 50s with pink hair. They were $25 each—I wasn't even drunk. They were just so cute that I bought two. I was 31. I left the rocks in a friend's car after leaving the market, and never saw them again.

- Yoho diabolo and fire twirling sticks from a market. I was like, 'I'll need these for my career as a street entertainer.' I sold them literally two days later. I had no ambition to be a street entertainer, but the lady who sold them to me was just so cool. (I do this heaps—buying stuff because I don't wanna let down the cool shop assistant.) They were $350. I told you I get swept up in the moment.

I have always wondered why I'm usually poor.

This list has sorted that out.

INTERVIEW

How awful are job interviews? They're like dating but with zero prospect of a free dinner. I've been to a few job interviews in my life and, in the interests of imparting all my wisdom, I thought I would compile a list of things not to say at a job interview. You're welcome.

- Sorry I'm late. Here's my resumé. I couldn't find a pen, so I used my own blood.
- Sometimes I get so mad, I just wanna kill a man, you know?
- I know you're interviewing me but you have a punchable face. I'm sure you get told that heaps.
- I'm sorry I haven't dressed in traditional work attire. I'm very drunk.
- What Christmas present do we get from the company? If it's a basic ham, I'm out.
- My old employer was awful—I hated her so much, I broke into her house and stole her TV and hummus.
- Can you guys be in my Boomerang? I'll write as the caption *interview feels*.
- Can my pet ferrets come to work? I have six, and five of them are sexually aggressive.

- I'm so much more productive if I have Mondays and Thursdays and Fridays off.
- I hate working. Will that be a problem?
- Legally, I have to tell you that I have a tendency to steal.
- I hate people; do I have to talk or be around people in this job?
- Oh, my penis face tattoo? I got it after I stabbed this guy as a dare.
- What's your policy re: Facebook use while working?
- I'm currently on meth. Can you speak a little slower?

INBOX

Because I work online, people can find me pretty easily and send me messages. Most people who write to me are really cool and lovely, and I genuinely love reading their messages. But occasionally I get super-creepy, weird emails. Here are a few I've received:

From: Andrew
If I win the lottery, will u marry me please? LOL. We can live together and you can wear pigtails.

Mate, you're a straight-up freak. But, I mean, sure, okay . . .

From: Greg
I don't want to come off as a gross older guy, but can I lick your hands?

Ooh. Hard pass.

From: Peter
Hi Tanya, I've recently moved back to Australia from England. I think you're gorgeous. This might sound weird, but I'd love to have a bath with you.

Who even has baths anymore?

From: Vlad
I find you very attractive. But only if you're Russian. Are you Russian? Because if you're not Russian I won't be attracted to you. Tanya is a Russian name, so you must be Russian. If you're not Russian I will feel like you have lied to me. I don't want to see you. You have betrayed me. You are not Russian.

I will be Russian away from you, Vlad . . . See what I did there? #worstjokever

From: Kale
You're banging for a 30-year-old. Can I fertilise one of your eggs?

You never replied. I want to fertilise you. Message back pls. Or follow me on Insta?

Hello. Are you going to let me fertilise you?

Fuck you.

Tempting . . .

From: Sam
If I buy you Nutella, will you be my in-house, pants-off lover?

I mean . . . maybe.

From: Taylor

If you have time, I would love a pic of your feet. Don't cut off the toes. I cant wait to see your toes.

Gross.

From: Riley

Youre more attractive in fake tan. I'm not being rude it's just a fact. Dont screenshot this and use it as a video. It's just that without it—you don't look good. Again, just a fact. I'm not bullying you. I just think that when you don't wear fake tan you don't look nice. I'm not a troll—I'm trying to help you. Please wear fake tan.

Gurl, I literally agree.

From: Kylie

Can you come to our charity run? I know that's a big ask, cause you don't really move. But you can just do a social media post?

I mean . . . Kylie knows my brand.

From: Tina

I'm so annoyed you're not lesbian. I watch all of your videos and think about your round boobs

Spoiler alert: they are less round, and more like irregular fried eggs on nails.

From: Karen

I don't think you're hot at all but you can be funny.

Thanks, babe.

From: Alan
I think your sweat would taste so good.

You sound balanced.

From: Kerry
I want to fly you to my home in Ireland so I can watch you closely.

Economy or business?

From: Chris
I hope you find someone. I think with all those chins, it will be hard.

Correct.

From: Corey
I saw you today. I took photos of you shopping in Coles. Don't worry, they're just for me.

Thanks so much, Corey. Chivalry is not dead.

From: Josh
I'm thinking of leaving my wife to be with you. I live in Texas but am willing to relocate. Can you give me an indication of whether or not this would be a good idea? If you're not keen, I'll just stay here.
PS Can you cook?

No to both.

From: Ben
My 9-year-old says you look like a man.

Well, I do have a moustache . . .

IMPOSTOR SYNDROME

I'm pretty sure I have impostor syndrome.

I think a lot of people feel this way. It's this feeling that I am constantly going to be called out: 'Tanya, we're onto you. We know you don't know what you're doing, mate . . . get out.'

I think I'm fooling people and soon they will find out I have no idea what I'm doing. I feel like I have slipped through the cracks. I feel like a fraud who's just waiting to be exposed any minute.

Writing this book is so strange for me. Again, a part of me thinks I fooled a publisher and this won't go to print because they will find out I'm actually making everything up as I go. I honestly am just waiting to be sent an email saying, *Sorry, no way would we publish you.*

I think so many people know this feeling. It comes from the negative self-chat. The loud voice in your head who tells you you're shit.

She will say on a loop:

'You don't deserve to be here.'

'You're a fraud.'

'One day, people will realise you have no idea what you're doing.'

'You're not funny.'

'You're not original.'

'You can't do anything of value.'

'You are so sensitive that it annoys everyone.'

'You are going to get fired, you're so bad.'

'You're a terrible role model.'

'You're not interesting.'

'You look gross in that outfit.'

'Why are you even talking?'

I don't really want to listen to her; she's just so loud. And she drowns out a lot of good things.

In fact, I really hate this voice. She has stuffed up a lot of opportunities for me, because of the times I have listened to and believed her.

I've been in a battle against this voice for years and I've realised I can't keep letting her win. She's won too many times. I have realised only I can make me, and I can break me, and I don't want to get in my own way anymore.

Now I'm trying to hear her as a thought, and not as a fact, and let what she says go. It's hard. I think that instinctively I'm inclined to self-hatred, instead of supporting and loving myself. I'm trying to change this habit and it's a hard one to break.

Conversely, I do have another voice inside my head.

It's soft and quiet—but equally powerful. Sometimes I can't hear her at all, but I can't silence her either.

She is the voice that, in my darkest hours, says: 'Don't give up. You're worthwhile; you are enough.'

She's been there since day one. She's always told me: 'Keep going, even if you can't afford to pay your rent.' She's the one who talks to me when I'm in a fog that makes it hard to care, or get motivated; when all I want to do is stay in bed; when I don't want to talk to anyone; when I don't want to leave the house; when the tears won't stop, and I find it hard to make sense of, or reason in, anything. She says: 'You will get through this; you have to. You will be okay. Keep going.'

That tiny voice has propelled me. That smallest, softest little voice, in what feels like eternal space, is why I am here.

Thank you, little voice.

INSTAGRAM

I'd like to use this entry to clear something up. I feel like there's something I should apologise for.

Here goes.

I'm really sorry about my Instagram.

I want to say sorry because, like many people on Instagram, I've chosen to show the best parts of my life. And if you follow me, you might be led to believe that my life is always *amazing*.

But that's not true. I just choose to show the coolest highlights. The angles that I hate the least.

I don't show how hard it can be.

I don't show how much anxiety I have about the things I do, and how terrifying I find it to be in the public eye.

I don't show you how housebound I really am.

I make it seem like my life is really easy and fun, and that I never have mornings when I wake up and feel like I can't get out of bed.

And I'm sorry. Because I always want to be honest and, while I haven't lied, I haven't shown you the whole story.

I'm sorry because I want you to know how hard it's been. Mostly, I don't want you to judge your success based on what people choose to post.

Just because someone appears a certain way on social media doesn't mean that's how they actually are. I know I've been guilty of looking at other people's Instagram accounts and comparing myself to them. *Why didn't I get invited to that event? Why didn't I get that opportunity? It must be because I'm terrible. Why aren't I as thin as her? She always look so busy and successful! How come she's always so happy? How does she have time to go to the beach? How does she have kids on top of her career? How does she manage it so well?* I assume that what I see in these pics is real. But it's not. I know it's not.

And I'm sorry.

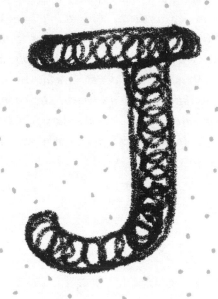

J
IS FOR...

JULES

The first year I made a video was 2015.

I'd wanted to make videos since 2012, but it took me three years to get my act together. WHY?!

First, because I'm lazy to my core. There's really nothing I enjoy more than sleeping. I know it looks like I work a lot, but if I'm not working—I'm sleeping.

Second, and most importantly, I waited because I was scared. *Really* scared. I didn't know where to start; I didn't know what to say. I didn't think I was going to be funny or entertaining or interesting. I just couldn't do it. So . . . I put it off, and off, for years.

Then one day, around June 2015, I paid my Italian friend Alex (I mention his ethnicity because he still owes me pasta and biscotti) to film and edit a presenting showreel for me. I planned, once it was done, to send it to Jules Lund.

'Why Jules?' I hear you ask. Great question.

When I was doing a short presenting course at NIDA, Jules was the poster child for TV presenting. Seriously, any time our teachers wanted to demonstrate how to present, they used footage of Jules. The guy was slaying it on *Getaway* and had gigs coming out of his ears. He was (and is) an incredible presenter.

It was terrifying to think of Jules watching my work, but I had a good feeling about it too. By that stage, I was doing radio in regional Queensland, and all I could think was, *Who do you think you are, sending bloody Jules Lund your showreel?* But I got his email from the network database, shut my eyes and hit send.

Obviously, I assumed I would never hear from him. *Why would he reply to me? He's so busy, and has way better things to do than write back to some rando.*

But he did. He wrote back.

I remember seeing his reply in my inbox.

I just about died.

1 new message.

Crap.

My first thought was: *Oh god, he hated it. This is hate mail.*

My second thought was: *He's mad at me for sending him a completely unsolicited email.*

My third thought was: *Wait. Have I turned the oven off?* (Unrelated.)

Then I calmed down, took a deep breath and opened the email.

It said: *Can I call you?*

He did, and we spoke for over an hour, and the upshot of what he told me was that I needed to create my own content, and not wait for a role, or some other opportunity, to present itself. I remember him saying: 'Tanya, you need to make two-minute videos that are really funny and have a bunch of personality. Just be you—you are your biggest asset. Put them on Facebook, and not on YouTube, and don't just say yes now, and hang up the phone and never do anything. Send me your first video.'

For me, this was one of those pivotal moments. I can still tell you what street I was on when I took the call, what I was wearing and what I was looking at. It was so life-affirming— somebody I had always looked up to believed I could do something, and cared whether I did.

So I made a video the next week. That video was called 'The Differences between 18 and 30' and it went viral.

Since then, Jules has been a mentor to me, as well as a co-worker. He's invited me on his shows, pushed me and encouraged me to keep going.

Jules, if you're reading, thank you for everything you've done for me. I wouldn't be writing this book without you, and I just hope I can be a 'Jules Lund' to someone else.

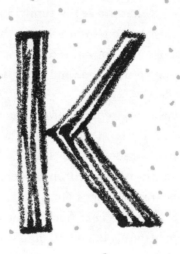

K
IS FOR...

KIDS

I *LOVE* kids.

I don't have any, but I just adore them, mainly because they have no filter and so say whatever they want.

Sometimes their honesty is hilarious. Other times, it's offensive and kinda mean. Like cry-yourself-to-sleep-in-a-bathtub mean.

Recently, I was in line at Kmart waiting to buy sheets and behind me was a mum with her kids.

The smallest girl, who looked to be about four, was wearing a sweet pink dress and had her hair in neat braids. She looked like a pageant child minus the spray tan. So innocent. So naïve.

She smiled up at me and I smiled back. Then she opened her mouth and said, 'Hey, missus. Are you pregnant in the bum?'

Um. Yep.

Are you pregnant in the bum?

For once, I had nothing to say.

I was shocked. (What a brilliant/heartbreaking way to describe my big bum.)

The little girl waited, obviously in need of an answer. The teenage cashier stared at me, wide-eyed, waiting to hear how I would react (probably so that she could tweet about what she'd just heard). Needless to say, the child's mother was mortified, and started apologising profusely.

But it was cool. Honestly. I laughed, and said, 'No (devil child), I just think Nutella and Cheezels are acceptable meals.'

She nodded, satisfied.

Kids saying the meanest things to me has become a bit of a theme in my life. Like:

'Tanya, why are your boobs so low?'

'Do you live in your car? Because you look like you live in your car.'

'When will you die?'

'Why aren't you married? Is it because you're too old now?'

'When is Tanya leaving our house?'

'Where are your kids? You should have kids. It makes me sad you don't have kids.'

'If you're not a mum, why do you have so many food stains on your clothes?'

'Can you fit on a motorbike? Are you allowed on a motorbike?'

Kids: back off. I love you, but your honesty is killing me.

Kids (Can I Be One Again, Please?)

How good was being a kid!?

Don't even answer. Don't. You *know* how good it was. The best.

No responsibilities.

No rent. No mortgage. You could have a tantrum whenever, wherever, and people would just be like, 'Ugh, she's a kid. It's what they do.'

Your mum packed your lunch every day, or—even better—gave you money for the canteen.

Best of all, you were praised all the time for every tiny little thing you did. At school, you would get stickers, or an award, for things like being a good listener or sitting up straight, or being the best clapper at assembly (which is not a thing).

I believe someone should give awards to adults to keep up the positive reinforcement. Certificates that read:

- I put away the laundry after putting it off for four weeks.
- I ironed today!
- I vacuumed even though I had 30 other things to do.
- I checked the mail and paid the bill that was in it without having a breakdown.
- I didn't punch my colleague in the face even though they were being a jerk in a client meeting.
- I had a meal with vegetables in it.

- I said I would do something and then followed through with it.
- I actually called my mum back.
- I was not socially awkward at my partner's work Christmas party.
- I washed my clothes and didn't just buy new undies from Coles on the way to work.
- I wore a supportive bra today.
- I went to the gym today.
- I showed self-control when there were bowls of chips at a party.

Kids on the Phone

While I like children (see above), I have no idea how to relate to children. Have you ever talked to a kid over the phone? It's excruciating. It's like they suddenly don't speak the same language as you and don't know *anything* about *anything*.

Recently, I had to call a friend (which is already The Worst because I hate using my phone as an actual phone— just text me) and her five-year-old daughter answered. Here is a re-enactment of my chat with this kid:

Me: Hello, Mia. How are you?

Mia: *(silence for ages)* Good *(barely audible)*.

Me: How's school going?

Mia: *(four years later)* Good.

Me: So, you like school?

Mia: Yes *(so, so quiet)*.

Me: What's your favourite subject? *(at this point, I'm thinking, Jesus Christ, this is worse than interviewing Justice Crew)*

Mia: Yes.

Me: Sorry? What? I can't hear you.

Mia: *(coughs)*

Me: *(racking my brain for what to ask next. What do kids like? Are Roll-Ups still a thing?)* So, how's Mummy?

Mia: Good *(whispers)*.

Me: What are you doing for Easter?

Mia: Good.

Me: Ahhh, okay. What's the Easter Bunny going to get you for Easter?

Mia: Eggs.

Me: Okay. Mia, can you put me onto someone else—literally anyone else?

Mia: *(suddenly full of life)* Yes. Mum, Tanya's on the phone! She wants to talk to you! Can we have hot dogs for dinner? Did you see my homework? I got 10 out of 10 on my artwork! MUM!

THIS IS WHY I NEVER CALL . . . ALWAYS TEXT.

Kids' Songs

Okay, so I've told you I'm an overthinker, and you already know I'm a weirdo. So, here goes.

Kids' songs: we all know them, we all listened to them when we were kids, and now we hear them as adults—but do we ever think about what we are singing?

I never did until one time I was babysitting and must have been in an overly analytical state.

First, can we talk about 'Hush Little Baby'?

Hush, little baby, don't say a word.

Papa's gonna buy you a mockingbird.

Who in their right mind is buying their child a mockingbird? I mean, seriously, how spoiled can you get? This is a kid who isn't going to be happy with a parrot, or some other cheap bird—it has to be one you need to import, and probably feed really expensive seeds.

And if that mockingbird won't sing,

Papa's gonna buy you a diamond ring.

Irrational jump. A bird to a DIAMOND RING!? WHY WOULD YOU BUY A BABY A RING!?

It's so impractical. Not to mention unsafe! Have you *met* a baby? They stick *everything* in their mouths. The next place you're gunna find that ring is in their nappy. Honestly, give them a piece of bread, some car keys and a cardboard box. Who's using diamond rings as a bargaining tool? It's so unrelatable.

Papa's gonna buy you a looking glass.

Okay, so this is a downgrade. From a diamond ring to a looking glass? Realistically, it should go from diamond ring to yacht. Not *looking glass*. What even *is* a looking glass and what kind of weirdo kid would want it? Whoever is writing this song is not thinking about the kid.

Papa's gonna buy you a dog named Rover.

Better. But at least let the kid name the dog.

And if that dog named Rover won't bark,

Hold up. Who gets rid of a dog that DOESN'T bark? That's a good thing! Barking dogs are currently one reason my parents are on the brink of divorce.

Papa's gonna buy you a horse and cart.

Look, it's a nice idea. Kids love ponies. I get it. But let's be real: how often are you really going to need a horse and cart? For the love of god, buy a Ford Focus.

And if that horse and cart fall down,
You'll still be the sweetest little baby in town.

So, after all that . . . nothing. Note to parents: you can't offer a diamond ring and then be like: 'You know what your real prize is? Being yourself.' No. That's not a prize. That's a fact. Give the kid her yacht.

And don't get me started on 'Johnny Works with One Hammer'. Have you heard this song? Oh my god.

Johnny works with one hammer,
One hammer, one hammer,
Johnny works with one hammer,
Then he works with two.

And so on.

So many questions.

First—what is he making that requires so many hammers?

When he went in to buy so many hammers, was the dude at Bunnings confused?

Who is Johnny? How *old* is Johnny? Is Johnny a child? If so, who is supervising this child?

And, most importantly, who ever needs more than one hammer? And who can use more than one hammer at a time? It's crazy.

Then there's this one:
Rub-a-dub-dub,
Three men in a tub,
And who do you think they were?
The butcher, the baker,
The candlestick-maker.

Wow. I mean, I've always thought there need to be more threesomes mentioned in kids' songs, don't you?

Kids' names

People name their kids weird things nowadays. Lion is a name, Tiger is a name, Bear is a name . . . oh my. (That was a terrible joke.)

I've met a Diamond, a Rainbow, an Ajax and a Crescendo.

I remember once bitching about these crazy names to a new guy at work. I should have got his name before I started. His name was Gotham.

People just make up names now but some people name their kids after things, like a friend of mine who loves Armani perfume, so named her daughter Armani, or a lady I used to work with who loved the city of Adelaide, and subsequently named her daughter Adelaide.

A friend on Facebook—which means, let's face it, a vague acquaintance I once worked with or someone I went to high school with who was in another grade to me—announced her pregnancy on Facebook and said, 'We're PREGNANT!!! We even have the name! She will be Paris! After where she was conceived!'

Imagine if everyone was named after where they were conceived?

I would be Beach; my high school best friend would be Wheelbarrow and her daughter would be Nightclub Toilet.

Kids Who Can't Speak Good

How cute is it when kids can't pronounce words properly?

It kills me.

Like when kids say 'pasketti', and not 'spaghetti'. Adorable.

I was playing with my boyfriend's four-year-old niece at a party recently when there was, er, an incident like this. Usually I make it a rule *not* to play with kids at parties, because, honestly, once you start playing with kids at a barbecue or party, you are *owned* by them till the function ends or they pass out from too much sugar, whichever happens first. And all I really want to do at these events is eat four thin Coles sausages, a few servings of potato bake and a sampler plate of whatever desserts are on offer. That's it. End of.

But this kid was cute, and I knew there would be dress-ups, so I gave it a shot and agreed to play superheroes with her. God, I am such a good girlfriend: there was so much cardio involved in this situation.

Anyway.

So, Adorable Little Girl runs up to me with a handmade cape and mask, and says proudly: 'Tanya! We're going to be girl superheroes. I'm going to be Super Girl, and you're going to be Fat Girl!'

I say nothing. Everyone at the barbecue turns to stare. Adorable Little Girl's mum rushes over, wine in hand and says: 'Oh my gosh, Tanya! I'm so sorry. Please don't be offended. Adorable Little Girl has always struggled pronouncing B. She means *Batgirl*! She just can't say the B.'

I have another B word I wanted to drop, but because Adorable Little Girl is four, I let it slide.

So there we are, running around the backyard, scaling the play equipment and saving the world from bad guys. The whole time, Adorable Little Girl is narrating the action.

'Come on, Fat Girl! Let's save the world, Fat Girl! Let's go, Fat Girl!'

I try not to let it get to me, but after 45 straight minutes of hearing 'Fat Girl' over and over, I'm having traumatic flash-backs to Year Nine.

Rationally, I know Adorable Little Girl doesn't mean anything by it. It isn't intentional. She isn't trying to screw with me. But it stings. My god, it stings.

And then, an hour into the game, Adorable Little Girl says: 'Right! Fat Girl! It's time to go find Ironman and Batman.'

Hold on.

What?

Batman?

Wait a sec.

'Did you say Ironman and Batman? You can say B?' I ask.

'Yeah,' she replies. 'You're just a fat girl.'

Oh man.

I definitely need new jeans.

(Friends with) Kids

Life is so different when you have a kid. I feel like parents have their own language. I don't have kids, but I know about parents because I'm pretty much the only one of my friends who doesn't have kids.

I'm that friend who is Aunty Tanya to everyone's kids. I'm the friend who is at every catch-up . . . but always forgets to bring what I was asked to. (But I *am* guaranteed to leave the barbecue with a dozen leftover rolls and several bags of Doritos.)

Catching up with my friends and their kids is always fun. I feel like I learn so much from them. Recently, I was at my friend's house for dinner. She and her husband have two kids, and because of that, we were having dinner at 5 p.m. Because that's when kids eat dinner. It's bizarre, but it does mean they're in bed by 7 p.m., which is when Mummy and Aunty Tanya break out the Sara Lee slab cake and go to town.

While the kids are getting into their pyjamas, I hear my friend's husband say to her, 'Honey, why is Ava's B-A-B-Y in the bin?'

'Oh, that's her old one,' says Amy.

'So do you want me to chuck the B-A-B-Y?'

'Yup,' says Amy. 'Also, if you want to have S-E-X later, can you please help me put the kids to bed now?'

At this point, I think, *This is fun; I can play along.*

'Did you get the S-H-O-P-K-I-N-S for Ava's friend's party?' Amy asks her husband.

'Ooh!' I say. 'What's Shopkins?'

The kids scream wildly and then start crying. 'Shopkins!' they wail.

Amy and her husband look at me like they may murder me.

'Tanya!' Amy hisses. 'We're spelling it out because we banned S-H-O-P-K-I-N-S from the house!'

Oops.

I had to leave.

It's been months and I still don't know what a Shopkins is. And I'm still in so much S-H-I-T with Amy.

REASONS MY FRIENDS WITH KIDS HAVE BAILED ON ME

Here are some reasons my friends (with kids) have bailed on me:

- 'My kids glued themselves together.'
- 'My kid ate money and now we're waiting for him to pass the $14 in coins he ate.'
- 'All three kids have nits and now I have nits too.'
- 'My kid put a pencil in her butt and now it's bleeding.'
- 'My kid vomited and then walked in the vomit, then walked around the house vomiting and walking it into the carpet, and now the vomit is making me vomit. Enjoy brunch, though.'

- 'My kid wrote on the walls with his own poo.'
- 'My kids put the cat in the washing machine and I turned it on.'
- 'My kid put my laptop in the toilet.'

L
IS FOR . . .

LONG-DISTANCE RELATIONSHIP

I was in a long-distance relationship for nine months. It was crap. Here are some damn good tips for y'all, 'cause Mama learned the hard way.

Thou shalt always tell someone if they are on speakerphone.
Honestly, it's bad enough calling your best girlfriend to whinge about your mutual friend, and it turns out you're on speaker, the mutual friend is there with them and they've heard everything.

It's even *worse* when you call your boyfriend and say, 'I can't wait to have so much sex with you,' (obviously, this was at the *very* beginning of our relationship) and he says: 'I should have said. I'm on speaker. At a family dinner.'

Thou shalt keep FaceTime to just you and your man.

You always think that when you're FaceTiming, it's gunna just be you and your man. But when your man is forgetful . . . that isn't always the case.

My boyfriend and I had designated times for our FaceTime chats, and sometimes we would plan for a . . . sexy FaceTime chat. Mostly they were just regular chats, though. To spice things up a little for one of our regular chats, I decided to wear something special: a see-through bralette and undie combo (again: very beginning of the relationship).

Unfortunately, my boyfriend's forgotten about our FaceTime session and agreed to babysit his nieces and nephews. As a special treat, he lets them answer the call.

'Hello, Aunty Tanya! Hello, Aunty Tanya's boobs!'

Thou shalt not send nudes. Ever.

I've never been the type to send nudes. It's not my style. But one time I did—my boyfriend is younger than me, and the relationship was long distance. It felt like the right thing to do.

Instead of sending a text message, though, I chose to send a few Snapchats, thinking it was the cool thing. They were pretty explicit. Unfortunately, I added them to my story, and didn't send them directly to my boyf.

Luckily, a friend texted me about 45 seconds after they'd gone up, so only about 10,000 people saw them. If they ever do resurface, though, I'll partly be devo and partly kind of okay because, honestly, they were explicitly *heaven*.

M

IS FOR . . .

MAKING NEW FRIENDS

Have you ever had to make new friends as an adult?

It's the strangest thing. It's like dating but weirder and worse.

I've had to make new friends as an adult A LOT. I've moved for work a lot, meaning I've moved to a town literally without anything but my clothes.

So far, I've done this three times as an adult—moved to a place where I knew *nobody*.

And because my jobs were in radio, where I was working odd hours—starting at 3.45 in the morning and finishing at 2 p.m., and sometimes working Saturday mornings too—it was even harder to connect with people. I couldn't stay out on a weekday past 7.30 p.m, and generally I've found that people who are under 75 or don't have small children don't like to have their dinner at 5 p.m.

Then there was the niggling question of exactly where to find these friends to have a 5 p.m. dinner with. *Is there a group? An app?* It's all so complicated. When you don't even have one friend, it's hard to be in an environment where you can find others. Generally, adults already have their friendship groups and they don't want to let any fly-by-night randoms into them. I get that. But it doesn't make it any easier for fly-by-nighters like me.

How to make friends in . . . Griffith

Ah, Griffith. Home to 30,000 people and 50,000 Italian restaurants. (Something like 80 per cent of the Griffith population is Italian, which was heaven, but also hell. I gained 10 kilos in six months.)

I lived on the main street in a one-bedder. It had no windows, floor-to-ceiling tiles and cost me $120 a week. It took me a month or so to figure out it must previously have been a meth lab. I'm not kidding—an ACTUAL meth lab. Oh well. At least it was clean.

Next to my block was an Italian-family-run fruit shop. The owner, Mimi, was around 55 and an absolute queen. Mimi knew I literally had no one to hang out with, so she let me hang out at the fruit shop with her almost every afternoon. Sometimes I'd help make juices or package up the cut fruit (sidenote: despite the pasta, this was the healthiest I've ever been because Mimi let me eat heaps of fruit. For once, I did not run the risk of scurvy). As our relationship progressed, I even went to Mimi's house, where she (tried to) teach me to make gnocchi. At Christmas, Mimi invited me to the fruit shop end-of-year party.

And the thing about having no friends is that once people *know* you have no friends, they reach out. Well, old people do, anyway. So, as well as Mimi, I had Judy, the 68-year-old receptionist at my radio station. Judy, her husband and I went on a road trip to see their elderly friend who lived two hours away. It was so lovely, but I mean . . . I was 26 years old, hanging on a Saturday with two senior citizens and their immobile elderly friend. We had a great chat about the war and how good solitaire is. But I am grateful. There should be more Judys and Mimis in the world. What wonderful women.

How to make friends in . . . Toowoomba

Toowoomba is just outside Brisbane. It's very conservative and has a lot of churches, but is also very pretty. I honestly loved T-ba. But it was hard to make friends there.

When I first started working in Toowoomba, my co-announcer was in his 40s with kids and a wife, and there weren't really any younger staff.

Weekends were the worst part of my week, especially when I first got there. As soon as I finished work on a Friday, a creeping sense of dread would come over me. *Two days alone*, I'd think. *What am I going to do to fill the time?!* After all, there's only so much time you can spend with your own mind, watching TV and flicking between the same four social media apps.

I wasted a lot of time in T-ba. I drove around a lot (I'm surprised I wasn't a person of interest to the police). I walked around the shops aimlessly, just because I wanted to be near other people.

I wasn't completely alone, though. I had: The Lady Who Did My Nails, The Lady Who Did My Spray Tans, and Some People Who Owned Shops And Occasionally Said Hi To Me As I Walked Past. To be honest, I would go get my nails, hair or tan done just so I could talk to someone. It would make me feel less alone.

I was drowning in isolation. People assumed that, because I was on air, I had heaps of mates. The truth was that I had nobody, and I'd often spend my weekends crying.

But towards the end of my time in T-ba, I did make a group of close friends. Actually, they were the best friends I'd had since high school. We all worked in the media, we were the same age, and they were just really great ladies.

They were the very definition of 'my people'. They weren't just people I hung out with because I couldn't find anyone else. They saved me.

When I left for Canberra, my heart was broken. I knew I'd be starting all over again and. more to the point, I'd be doing it without my Toowoomba girls. I didn't want to be alone again. I wanted to feel safe and comfortable around people I knew.

How to make friends in . . . Canberra

I started my job in Canberra in January, and because I didn't want to go through what I'd been through in Griffith and

Toowoomba, a few months later I put a video on Facebook, basically asking for friends.

I said something like: 'Hi, I'm Tanya! This is my house in Crace [a Canberra suburb]. As you can see, there's no one else here. I live alone and I don't have any friends in Canberra. DM if you want to hang out.'

I thought that maybe I'd get . . . I don't know . . . six replies? I got close to 25,000.

Then the whole thing kind of went viral. My little Facebook video was on National Nine News, Mamamia, news.com.au, *The Morning Show*, *Studio 10*, and more. *The Project* sent out a crew to film what was going to happen. It was pretty scary, because this wasn't some bid to make the news: it was a very real story. I *was* alone. But once I opened up about how hard it was to be alone, something amazing happened—other people started talking about it too.

People rang us on air and told their stories. They said things like:

- 'It's really hard being alone on the weekends. I've tried making friends at work but everyone already seems to have their clique. I feel really left out.'
- 'I just heard you on the radio talking about the difficulties of finding friendships in Canberra, and almost started crying. I've been here for seven years now and I don't have any friends.'
- 'I moved to Wagga two years ago for my husband's work. I've found it so difficult to make friends, so I totally get

you. I spend most of my time on Netflix . . . it's great but it doesn't talk back.'

🖤 'OMG . . . I hate the weekends too. I have no friends either! I moved here four years ago and I can't break into a friendship group or make new friends . . . so I've given up trying.'

HOLY SHIT—I THOUGHT IT WAS JUST ME!!?

It was so comforting to know that I wasn't alone, but it was also really sad to think so many people were feeling the same way.

We ended up having a few mass-friend dates in Canberra, which people went along to—alone—in the hope of meeting some new people who might turn into friends. It was amazing. And while not everyone came away with a best mate, there were plenty of people who made real connections.

After being so inspired by all the connections being made around me, I had the confidence to reach out to a guy called Jamie, who was a friend of a friend who'd told me I needed to meet him when I moved to Canberra. I held off on contacting him because I was scared. *What if he doesn't want to meet me? What if he doesn't like me? Meeting a stranger in a café is weird. I'm so socially awkward. I hate going to places alone.*

It sounds like a small thing, but for me, at that time, it was a big step: I asked him to have a coffee.

He said he would love to.

When I met him, I was like YES. YES! YES! . . . we were just a good fit. There is a lot to say for 'finding your tribe'. Jamie was my tribe. An eccentric *Will & Grace* and musical theatre-loving, Disney-obsessed weirdo. He was me, but with a penis and more coordination.

He's one of my closest friends to this day.

The lesson

Um, right. The lesson. I guess the lesson is that you've gotta put yourself out there and get out of your comfort zone. You've gotta say yes more often than not, even if it's uncomfortable. Because what's worse? Being slightly terrified but then gaining a friend? Or never putting yourself out there, and constantly being miserable, and alone, and watching other people's lives on Facebook as you seethe with jealousy?

And look, sometimes you don't wanna be with people all the time. Sure. I get that. As I get older, I NEED more alone time to recharge. But you need to know you have someone to call if you want to go out; to text, when it's a shit day at work so you can vent; or if you're really needing help.

But there's another lesson here that's not just about *you* and *me*: if someone new starts at work who's just moved to town, don't assume anything. Don't assume they're okay or have heaps of friends, or think, *This is too hard for me, I have a lot going on.* Just invite them out. You could help someone. A lot. Sometimes people just need someone to download the day to; just one person to make them feel less alone. Invite them to drinks. Do it for me. Please. I promise it'll work out.

MIGRAINES

Anyone else suffer from migraines? I do. I suffer from *really bad* migraines. The fact that I'm able to work on top of having these migraines is nothing short of a miracle. I'm getting better but I've been in a lot of pain, a lot of the time. Sometimes the pain has been so bad that I couldn't see.

I've tried everything to get rid of them. You name it, I've tried it.

The one thing I've found that works (besides botox in my skull—google it, it's a real thing) is remedial massage. The masseuse 'unlocks' trigger points in your neck and it helps a lot.

My old, amazing, masseuse packed up shop though, so I was in the market for someone new. I googled 'remedial massage' and called the one that was the first result on the list (probably a mistake, looking back).

A woman answered the phone. Immediately, as soon as she says, 'Hiiiii, this is Donna,' I know who this woman is. She definitely wears too many rings, has beaded curtains and shops at Tree of Life.

She has a deep, breathy voice. She sounds like she's in her mid-40s, has just done a nude yoga course (as the teacher, not the student), has several toe rings and is definitely a vegan.

Already I know this is not what I need, but I proceed.

'Uh, hi,' I say. 'Do you do remedial massage?'

'Ah yes,' she says, breathy AF. 'I can.'

I can? What does that even mean?

'So do you do trigger point massage?' I ask this question knowing full well she won't/can't.

'Ah, sure,' says Donna. 'If you've had it done before, you can just show me.'

Jesus Christ.

'Can I use my health insurance?'

'Sometimes; it depends if the machine is working.'

Of course.

'Right,' I say, feeling a bit desperate but also wondering why I don't just hang up. 'I just have really bad migraines.'

'Well,' says Donna, suddenly all knowing, 'if you have migraines, you don't need massage. What you need is the Elixir of Life. I invented it. It's a serum of water and salt.'

So, saline? You invented saline?

'When are you free?' I ask, knowing I would rather eat my own hand than be anywhere near this woman.

'I'll have to call you back about that. It all depends on my husband.'

What does that even mean?

'Where exactly are you?' I ask, expecting it to be a dungeon where she keeps both crystals and human skin.

'I operate out of my house. You'll see it from the street, there's a beaded curtain at the door.'

Called it.

'I have to go into a meeting,' I say. 'I'll call you back.'

I didn't call back.

I did, however, get a $2 massage from a chair in a Westfield. It didn't help my migraines but it also didn't cost me my life, so that's a win.

MASSAGE

Donna is not the only bizarre experience I've had with a massage therapist, of course.

There is something about nudity combined with rubbing and strangers that just makes for awkwardness.

When I was in Bali, I was living in massage parlours because it's, like, $7 an hour for a full-body massage AND IT IS AIR-CONDITIONED (see the entry on Bali).

I got so many massages. Too many, really. I was *too* loose. By the end of the trip, I was just loose muscle hanging around in skin.

But on my last day, I thought I'd try something different— a scrub at a fancy spa recommended to me by a friend. Instead of the usual $7, it was $40 for 40 minutes of exfoliating goodness. *All right*, I think. *Live.*

From the outside, the spa looked beautiful. Rock pools, white everything, sheer curtains blowing in the breeze. Bliss. It looked expensive, and I felt like I was a very fancy lady, even though I had sweat patches under my boobs.

Then I walked into the room. And it was like the set of *Saw*.

Dark cement. Everywhere. In the centre, there was a cement table. The floor was saturated with god knows what. I could barely see anything.

The beauty therapist asked me to lie nude on the table. She gave me a paper G-string to cover myself, and it broke.

After scrubbing the shit out of my legs and back, the woman said, 'Miss, can you turn around?'

Oh god.

Now I was on my back, with my boobs facing the ceiling—or, if we're being honest, sitting in my armpits.

She started scrubbing the front of my legs, my arms, neck; then stomach and, finally, my boobs.

Annnnnd I'm officially uncomfortable.

While she was scrubbing my boobs, I smiled to break the tension, because it was just so awkward. Unfortunately, she seemed to misunderstand the smile as meaning: *Keep going! I'm loving this!* because she then continued on the boobs for 20 minutes.

So: 40-minute scrub, 20 minutes of which were spent solely on my boobs.

I thought she was going to scrub my boobs *off.* At least the nipples, anyway.

When it finally ended, I had two thoughts:

Shit, my boobs are red.

and

I got more intimate with this beauty therapist than I did with my boyfriend this holiday.

And while we're talking about cheap, who doesn't love a bargain? If I can get something for 20 per cent off the already reduced price, I am in heaven. Yes, I'm cheap. In fact, I pride myself on being able to get good discounts and/or bargains.

But there is such a thing as something being TOO CHEAP or too much of a bargain!

I hear you say, 'NO WAY! LIES! HERESY! HOW?' Okay, here's how . . .

A month or so ago, I hurt my shoulder.

Was it an injury from exercise? Or was it from an afternoon sleep on a jar of Nutella that was lodged in my bed? Who's to say . . . ?

So, I went to get a massage. It was a rainy old day in Sydney and, being cheap, I was not looking for anyone who had a booking system. I just wanted to get in and out, with limited eye contact. I saw a massage place down a skanky back alley in the city (in this same alley, a man was clipping his toenails with his teeth). But! I pushed on, and into the massage place, because the sandwich board on the main street said *$13 for half hour massage*. And THAT was what I wanted! Cheap!

I walked into a dimly lit, musty place. I don't think this place had been cleaned, literally, ever. 'Summer Rain' was playing, softly. It was not okay. But before I could leg it, the woman who was working there came right up to me and said, 'Can I help you?' Oddly, she was holding a full box of doughnuts.

There was not a soul in there besides this woman and me. I was their one and only customer. (Legit, I may have been the only customer they had ever had, and the shop looked like it had been there for at least 15 years.) There was no way I could have walked in by accident, so I felt obliged to get a massage.

After confirming that $13 was the correct price, I lay down, topless. The lady came in, eating one of the doughnuts and texting (professional), and nonchalantly asked me, 'What pleasure do you like?'

Oh. I see. At this point, my inner monologue had gone ballistic: *OMG, the 'massage' is $13, everything else is extra! You idiot! What are you doing??! This was obviously too cheap! Get out! Get OUT! This is an ending you don't need to pay for!*

Outwardly, I asked, 'Sorry, what now?'

She replied, 'What pleasure do you like?' still with a doughnut in her mouth.

At this point, I didn't know what to do. I started to put my top back on. 'I don't need a massage that badly . . . what kind of massage is this?' I said to her.

The lady put down her phone and cleared her throat of doughnut, laughing as she said, 'No no . . . what PRESSURE do you like?'

Ohhhh, pressure! NOT pleasure. (Heart rate returns to normal.)

Before I got a chance to leave, she started the massage, and it wasn't bad, to be honest. But the whole time, I was thinking: *Good lord. How will this end!? What's going to happen at the end of the massage?*

After half an hour, my ordeal was over. I paid my $13 and I left. Would I do it again? No. It was too cheap.

She gave me one of her doughnuts, though.

Which, oddly, was a happy ending for me.

MEDIUM

In regional radio, you always get weird and wonderful people in the studio. There's everyone from the overly chatty local

Harvey Norman franchisee, to the reptile park rangers who come in every school holiday to spruik their shows.

Oh, and there's always a psychic or medium in the mix. ALWAYS. When I was working in Griffith, we got a psychic on the show to help us identify whether or not a particular local landmark was haunted.

She entered the studio while a song was playing and the first thing she said was, 'Oh my, you have a face for radio.'

Without thinking, I shot back, 'For a medium, you look more like a large.' We never did find out if the place was haunted.

MATERNITY CLOTHES

I hate clothes shopping.

Hate it.

I hate browsing for stuff in shops while the hot chicks who work there and who wear clothes effortlessly, and who are so cool and unknowingly intimidating, watch me.

I hate trying clothes on too, because nothing makes you feel more horrific than a change room with four mirrors, so you can see yourself at every angle. Nobody needs that!

I also hate clothes shopping because . . . again . . . I'm cheap. Really cheap.

So I wear the same clothes over and over again. Not hyperbole. I wore the same four tops for three years. If you have seen any of my videos, you will know I literally wear the same four tops.

Anyway, one day I thought I'd better add a fifth top to the rotation and psyched myself up to go clothes shopping. As luck would have it, the first shop I went into had these cute oversized black-and-white-striped jersey cotton tops. They were super oversized, which meant I didn't need to try them on! WIN.

They looked cute: WIN.

They were *five bucks*: WIN.

So I bought five—five—tops for 25 bucks. WIN WIN WIN . . . and I didn't have to try any of them on. (Sing 'Hallelujah'.)

I headed home and changed into one of my brand-new tops to go out for dinner. While I was lining up to order at a Mexican place with my housemate, I saw a guy I had a massive crush on standing behind me.

'Hey, Tanya,' he said.

'Heyyyyyyy,' I said, trying to sound like a normal, rational person, and failing.

'Ah, your tag is still on your shirt, tag dag!' he said. He ripped it off and handed it back to me. I looked down at it. *Maternity*, it said. IN MASSIVE LETTERS.

'I didn't know you were pregnant!' he said.

Oh god.

'No!' I say. 'No, I just bought this top on sale. No, no. Not pregnant.' I tried to rescue the situation, but just spewed out word vomit while overcompensating. 'I mean, who would have sex with this? Literally no one. I've tried and everyone's like, "No thanks." Literally not pregnant. I am anti pregnant, if anything. I just thought it was oversized. I'm still single. Still single. Very, very single. Like, desperately single. Wearing a maternity shirt . . .'

Yes! Smooth.

Nothing turns a guy on more than desperation and hearing just how undesired you are by other men.

He laughed awkwardly.

I ordered double Mexican and left.

Strangely, I never saw him again.

I have since bought more of what I thought were flowy/ oversized shirts online and later found out they were maternity wear.

Three years later, at 32 and with no children, I currently own 13 maternity shirts and two pairs of maternity jeans. I am not proud of myself.

But I am so comfortable—10/10 would recommend.

N

IS FOR . . .

NUDITY

Anyone else like to be nude?

You might be surprised to hear this but . . . I love being nude. LOVE IT. It's who I am.

Here's why: you don't have to worry about clothing not fitting if you're not wearing any. It's just nice to have no restrictions. I feel like my jeans are always cutting into my tummy, my undies are too tight, the underwire in my bra always rubs and my tops just sit weirdly. I feel like I'm always pulling at and adjusting what I'm wearing. So, I'm always uncomfortable in clothes, meaning that without the clothes I feel free and comfortable. Honestly, if you're not nuding it up, you should be.

(Sidenote: if you're a bigger-titted lass, you will need to hold them up after a while because they will hurt, gurl. Nudity is hard for big-boobed ladies.)

I'm a home nude, though. I should clarify that I'm not a nudist. I would never go to a nude beach, or just any beach, because: sand and people. I'm all about being post-shower nude. Have a shower, then have a few nude hours.

I've also gotten into the habit of making dinner nude. Which is great, but not if you live in a high-rise apartment and you forget that your windows shades are up and open. (Like I said, this nudity is for me, not anyone else; despite the fact I have given up, I do have some shame. Some.)

One night, I'd been nude cooking and dancing for a good two hours before I realised my window shades were up.

I looked across at the building next to mine. Hoping no one had seen. Bugger. A cat in a window was making eye contact.

But it was okay. It was just a cat. It felt weird that a cat was watching me dance and cook nude. But it was just a cat.

Before I got the chance to shut my blinds, a lady grabbed the cat and we made eye contact.

I was full-bush, full-frontal nude. That poor woman.

She closed her blinds while shaking her head at me.

Fair enough: I had been shaking my boobs at her all afternoon . . . and, now I think about it, all year. I don't think I ever closed those shades.

Shit—I did a lot of bending over.

The woman moved out three weeks later. I wondered if my nudity had anything to do with it. Probably, because she left a note on my car:

Close your blinds.

NORMAL

Have you ever thought something you did was normal until you said it out loud and other people were like: 'Oh no. That is definitely not normal.'

It will probably not be a huge shock to learn that this happens to me a lot.

Like the time I thought everyone still slept with their childhood bear. I found out this was not the case when I was 30. Surrounded by a large group of people.

Then there was the way we celebrated birthdays in my Year Two class at school. Again, I thought this was all par for the course. A regular day at an Aussie school. Then I told my cousin about it years later and she was like: 'Ah, yeah. If that happened in a school now, it would be an international news story.'

Our teacher would sit on a chair, and we in the class would sit with our legs crossed on the mat in front of her. She would mark the roll, read to us and sing to us. So far, so normal, yeah?

When someone in our class had a birthday, we would celebrate. Again: normal.

(Sidenote: don't you think it's weird that when you're little, birthdays are such a big deal, but as you get older, it's like, 'Ugh, birthdays are the worst'? What happens to us?)

Anyway. Birthdays. When it was someone's birthday, some-times we had a cake, and obviously we sang 'Happy Birthday' to the kid. Normal, normal. Also, if it was your birthday, the teacher would give you a chocolate stick. (Relatively normal.) How cool is that!?

Looking back, I think she made them herself. I didn't really think a lot about it, though. I was seven. It was chocolate. Heaven.

(Another sidenote: I wish I could go back to a time when I was so delighted by these little things. I remember being so excited I could have cried about a McDonald's Happy Meal. And remember Christmas when you were a kid? It was actual magic. You couldn't sleep the night before, it was so huge. You were treated like a god and you loved every minute. Now think of Christmas as an adult—not even day drinking helps. Now, there is literally nothing that makes me feel even one per cent of that amount of joy. You try so hard to recreate how you felt as a kid but, no matter what you do, it's just not the same.)

Anyway, I digress.

There we were, sitting cross-legged in front of our teacher, singing 'Happy Birthday'. Normal. And when the song was over, we would get . . . birthday smacks. So, not normal.

Yeah. Birthday smacks. Not *snacks*. Smacks.

It wasn't painful and it wasn't done in a mean way. Weirdly, it was . . . loving. We all really loved it and looked forward to it.

(This is a real story, by the way. It sounds fake, I know.)

The teacher would bend us over her legs, in front of the whole class, and smack us for every year we'd been alive. So, if you were turning seven, you'd get seven birthday smacks and one for good luck. That one—the last one—was big. And we'd all count along: 'One! Two! Three! Four! Five! Six! Seven! And one for good luck!'

Then we would all clap for the birthday boy or girl, and class would continue. Again, normal.

Wow. It seemed bad when I was recounting it to my cousin, but it's worse in print.

Sorry.

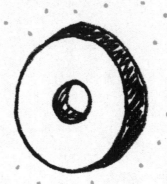

O
IS FOR...

OVERTHINKING

I'm an overthinker. Yep. Shocker. It's my worst personality trait. To anyone who knows me personally, I'm sorry! I know it's really annoying.

If you're an overthinker like me, you'll know that it means you're constantly reassuring yourself. *It's okay,* you think. *They probably aren't answering their phone because they're at work. There's probably a very simple explanation. It's not because they hate you! Calm down. It's okay. It's okay!*

But the overthinker in you thinks: *No! Look at when they were last on Facebook. Six minutes ago! You called them twice in that time and they didn't answer but they were clearly on their phone! They're definitely ignoring you because they hate you. Think about everything you could have done wrong and why they could possibly be mad at you.*

THE DIFFERENCE BETWEEN OVER-THINKERS AND NORMAL PEOPLE

On receiving text messages

Overthinker: They only put one kiss at the end where they normally put two or three they are mad at me. What did I do wrong? They hate me. Oh my god. What did I do? Was it something I said when I was with them last? I'm gunna screenshot this and send it to Mum . . . should I text them and ask why they are mad? I have lost a friend. I feel sick. Why? What's wrong with me? What did I do? If she doesn't text me straight back, she seriously hates me. Okay, let me run through this another 45 times to see if I can get a new understanding.

Normal Person: Cool, see you at 4 p.m.

Should I buy this hat?

Overthinker: I love this hat. Should I buy it? It's expensive, but I haven't bought myself anything in ages. At the same time, do I really need to reward myself? Mmm. I could wear it in summer, but what about winter? That's a whole season where I won't be getting any wear out of it. Maybe it's a waste. And where will I put it? Do I have any space for new hats? You know what? It doesn't look *that* good on me. Okay, that's it: I hate this hat.

(*Ten minutes later*)

But what if I *don't* buy it and then I regret it and come back to buy it and it's sold out?

Normal Person: Cool hat. I'll buy it.

Where should we go for dinner?

Overthinker: I don't know what I feel like. Thai might be good. Also KFC. But then I know I'll feel like something sweet later. Do I even want to eat? I don't know. Ugh, I hate picking what to eat. Subway could be good. Can I eat at home? What's the weather like? Maybe soup? But then what if I order it and immediately want pizza? No pizza. I'm trying to be healthy. So maybe salad. No—I can't have salad. I just remembered I hate salad.

Normal Person: I'll have the schnitty, please.

P

P

IS FOR...

PROCRASTINATING

Ways I have procrastinated while writing this book

- Told myself it was okay to do nothing on the book that night because I'd wake up early and write. I did not.
- Went shopping for hours to 'look for writing inspiration'. I mean . . . I *was* looking, but not for inspo. It was for shapewear because I ate so many marshmallow Santas while writing this book.
- Hung out with my friends for 'content' but didn't get a single idea from them.
- Slept in till the early afternoon to try to 'rest my brain'. I did feel rested but I also did not do any work after I woke up.

- Constantly texted friends during the writing process, in the hope they would have a crisis that I would a) need to help them with, and b) be able to write about later. Didn't happen.
- Constantly told myself I would write after 'one more episode of *RuPaul's Drag Race*'. I did not do it even after watching nine seasons of *RuPaul's Drag Race*.
- Justified being on Instagram as 'research'.
- Told myself I *needed* food breaks to write at my optimum, but they would be seven hours long and in another city.
- Sat on the toilet, and went between Snapchat, FB, Instagram, YouTube and various other apps . . . for 30 minutes.
- Wrote a 'P is for procrastinating' chapter.

PARENTS

I need my parents to help me with pretty much everything because—and this should be obvious if you've read up to this point—I can't be an adult without supervision and assistance.

Moving house is massive for anyone, but especially when you don't know how to unplug a washing machine or whatever. The way I don't. So my parents—bless them—have come and helped me every time I've moved house. Which, again, if you've read up to this point, you'll know is a lot.

When I moved into my unit in Canberra, I realised that I didn't own a TV. For years, I'd been watching *Family Guy* DVDs on my laptop, and filling my nights cooking/baking/microwaving nude.

So, of course I made my parents come with me to buy my first TV (at age 30). Deep down, I guess I still feel like I can't be trusted to do big things without a 'real' adult present.

My dad, who is 60, is much more technologically savvy than me. He suggested I get a smart TV so I could connect to wi-fi, and stream Netflix and whatnot. Great. (In other ways, he is exactly like *your* dad when it comes to technology, though—he has no idea what the 'cloud' is and has no interest in learning.)

'Your mother and I are using our smart TV to watch *Making a Murderer*,' he tells me. 'You'd love it, it's really great.'

'Okay, Dad,' I say, half-listening, half-scrolling on my phone, half-hoping he'll offer to put this new smart TV on the family credit card.

'Yep,' Dad continues, proudly, 'your mother and I pretty much Netflix and chill every weekend now.'

I look up.

'Yeah . . . that doesn't mean what you think it means, Dad.'

'Tanya. I know what it means, and your mother and I are doing it . . . every weekend.'

I'm almost laughing now, but I manage to hold it together. 'No, Dad. Netflix and chill doesn't mean you're watching TV and chilling out. It's an internet thing. It means . . . something else.'

Dad gives me a funny look. 'I know what it means, Tanya.'

I shoot him back an even funnier look. Not 'ha-ha' funny. Like 'I don't want to have this conversation' funny.

'Dad. Stop.'

He cocks his head to the side and nods. 'Every weekend, Tanya. Every weekend.'

WHEN MY MUM TEXTS ME

Recently, I got a new brow artist and now my brows look amazing. #humble

I sent a pic to my mum—I wanted her to see my heaven eyebrows.

Look at my eyebrows, Mum. How good do they look?

Mum writes back: *Eyebrows on fluke.*

No, Mum, I type. *It's fleek. Eyebrows on fleek.*

It's not the first time she's taken slang and completely mangled it.

She told me that at a Rod Stewart concert, she was in the 'MASH PIT'. Gurl, first, it's 'mosh pit' and, second, there is no way there was anything remotely like a mosh pit at a Rod Stewart concert.

Once I texted Mum while I was drunk. *Should I keep drinking, Mum?* (Obviously, if you have to ask, the answer is *no*.) But Mum replied, *Why not, Tanya? YOGO.*

YOGO?

No, Mum, I texted back. *It's YOLO.*

Nope. Mum insisted it was YOGO. So, whenever she texts me encouraging words, I now have a sudden craving for chocolate custard.

WHEN I TEXT MY MUM

Someone rear-ended me. What do I do?

What's my tax file number?

Can I borrow $70?

I'm sick. How do you make a doctor's appointment?

How long do I boil an egg?

What's the meaning of life?

My poo has a weird texture. Is it normal? Wait, I'll send you a pic.

I have a slight cough. Is that a sign of meningococcal?

How long do I defrost chicken for?

How do I get a home loan?

Can I borrow $100? I'll pay you back.

How do I get vomit out of curtains?

I have this mucousy cough. I just sent you a pic of the mucus.

I'm moving interstate. Can you help do everything, please?

Can you take a sick day and do this random thing with me because I don't wanna do it alone?

Mum, I have to do a bond clean and it's not clean unless you clean it. What are you doing Thursday?

Mum, can you make my bed? It's just better when you make it. That's a compliment!

Mum, I can't teach you how to use the computer anymore. Stop double-clicking everything.

Hey, where's my childhood doll? I haven't thought or asked about her in 10 years but I need her right now.

Can I borrow $250? I promise I'll pay you back this time.

Mum, when I get home, can you make me some toast?
I like the way you make it.

How do I turn the washing machine on?

Can you pay my rent? I will def pay you back. Serious!

Mum, what setting do I put the washing machine on for linen?

How do I handwash something? Can't you just do it?

Mum, can you sew a button onto my top?

Can I borrow $400? I'll pay you back! (I swear, I owe my parents $300 grand . . . not even an exaggeration.)

 # WEIRD SHIT PARENTS DO

As I've said, most of my friends have kids, and, honestly, they do some weird shit. Here's a sample:

They make fake phone calls
'If you don't eat your dinner, I'm calling your dance teacher and telling her you're not doing the concert.'
(*Picks up phone, makes dramatic, but fake, phone call to teacher, child cries.*)

They time you doing the most boring shit
'Go clean up your room! I'll time you.'

'Get ready for school! I'll time you.'
'Get Mum a wine! I'll time you.'

They can have two conversations at the same time
'Yeah, I can definitely do lunch at Grill'd. DON'T LICK THAT! Do you wanna do 12 or one? DON'T RIDE THE DOG! I can probably pick you up on the way. PUT YOUR UNDIES BACK ON! We could do somewhere with a woodfire pizza? STOP KISSING THE DVDS. Tanya, I have to go—GET OUT OF THE CAT FOOD, IT'S NOT FOR YOU TO EAT! YOU HAVE FRUIT RIGHT THERE!—I'll pick you up in 20.'

If they have two kids, they make sure everything is the same
Me: Who wants the pink Easter egg and who wants the blue?
Friend: Tanya, if you don't have two pink Easter eggs for my two girls, this will end in World War Three.
Me: No, it won't (*laughing*).
(*World War Three commences.*)

They lie. Just straight-up lie.
'Oh no! We can't go to McDonald's. They're closed. I know, it *says* they're open 24 hours but, trust me, they're closed. Oops, now we've driven past it, so we can't double-check.'

'Sorry! We can't watch *Frozen*. The DVD player and Netflix are broken. But they still work for adult shows.'

'The Easter show? No, they're not doing that this year. They only do it once every . . . 10 years. I think.'

MY MUM CAN'T COOK

My mum doesn't cook. She can't. She hates it. I mean, aside from toast, she is physically incapable of assembling a meal. She just can't be bothered. Which I totally respect. The woman had three kids and a job. Instead of feeding us, I don't know, chicken curry or pasta with meatballs, we would have fun, exotic meals like:

- SAOs. Just SAOs. 'Put whatever on them, kids.'
- Hot dogs . . . 'But we don't have frankfurts!' . . . so we're having a long bread roll for dinner.
- Sometimes tacos, but Mum would always forget the mince and the cheese and the lettuce and the tomatoes and the salsa and the sour cream.
- Fish fingers and carrots (that's not a meal, woman!).
- Party pies—and only party pies. Microwaved.
- Mum's frittata, which would be eggs, sweet potato, broccoli, peanuts and marshmallows, or whatever was in the cupboard.
- Burnt garlic bread dipped in salsa (. . . like, that was the whole meal).
- Sometimes we would have 'tapas', which was just anything in the fridge on one plate. You'd have, like, half a sausage, spaghetti bolognaise, cornflakes and an apple.

As a consequence, I can't cook either.
(NB: The truth has been stretched here . . . sorta.)

Q

IS FOR . . .

QUEENS WHO INSPIRE ME

- Tina Fey: Tina is a jack of all trades and a master of all. She is an incredible writer and performer. I'm in awe of what she has created. Game changer.
- Rebel Wilson: She's a killer confident Aussie! She moved to LA with nothing and made it huge. She took her destiny into her hands and made it work. She's a hustler and she has mega talent.
- Megan Mullally: Karen from *Will & Grace*. Singer, dancer, comedian. So talented. She has some of the best comedic timing in the world. This woman's style has informed a lot of my tone in comedy.

- Kristen Wiig: I mean . . . her timing and characters are flawless. She's a master improviser as well.

- Kate McKinnon: I can't get enough of her. She has that X factor. She's a fearless performer who really cares about the craft.

- Melissa McCarthy: Bow down to Queen Melissa. I mean, she's just funny. She is just so effortlessly funny. She doesn't take herself too seriously and I love that.

- Abbi Jacobson and Ilana Glazer: These ladies hustled their arses off. *Broad City* is like nothing else. They love and support other women in comedy. Praise to Abbi and Ilana.

- Magda Szubanski: Growing up, there was no one like me on TV. At least, no one I related to. Except for Magda. She let herself look gross for the sake of the character. She didn't care about pretty, she cared about funny. She's special.

- Lilly Singh: Lilly is the best comedy creator on digital. No one compares. Lilly has a massive heart. She cares about her craft and cares about people. She always shouts out other women and smaller creators. Respect.

Here are some kings I look up to too.

- Ricky Gervais and Stephen Merchant: I have a picture of Ricky Gervais on my wall. *The Office*, *Extras* and *An Idiot Abroad* are three of my fave comedies. Both these men have phenomenal timing and comic sensibilities.

- Seth MacFarlane: He's the creator of *Family Guy*, and some jokes are taken too far in that series. But I mean . . . he's a genius. He finds funny in a different place. Like calling an ostrich Dave and making him a recently divorced gay caricature. I love *Family Guy* and I love how many musical references and songs are in it.

- Chris Lilley: *We Can Be Heroes* is one of my other fave narrative comedy TV shows. He broke the mould, and created an incredible legacy. He is so original. His characters are so well layered and constructed. I think Chris Lilley is an absolute genius.

- Sean Hayes: I mean . . . Jack in *Will & Grace* was obviously written for him, but what he did with that role was incredible. The timing . . . the delivery. Incredible.

- Rhys Nicholson: One of Australia's best stand-up comedians. He's smart, he's hilarious, his comedy is well crafted and he breaks the mould. He's so different. A sensational comic talent.

QUOTES

I have become 'that person' who is into quotes. The worst kind of quotes—motivational quotes.

And yes, I hate myself for it. Ugh. I never thought I would be that person, but here we are.

To be honest, though, I only have one quote that I really live by. The rest I found on the 'gram, like all normal people under 40.

Ready? Here it is:

IT'S BETTER TO DO IT AND BE TERRIFIED THAN NOT DO IT AND BE TERRIFIED.

I should preface this story by telling you that, since high school, I had wanted to do stand-up. But I was so terrified, I just couldn't. I was forever the class clown, always telling jokes even when I was a kid . . . I knew I wanted to do it. But every time I would even consider putting my name down at an open mic stand-up night, I would get so anxious. Like throw-up-in-a-bag anxious, like heart-attack anxious, like diarrhoea anxious. Even if the gig was 12 weeks away, I would feel that anxiety for the whole time leading up to it. Just the thought of it made me sick. So it just didn't seem worth it.

By the time I was 24, I was gaining confidence. I bought a microphone stand—no microphone, just the stand. I would practise in my bedroom for hours. It still scared the hell out of me, even though it was just me in my own room. It was like no other fear.

But I digress.

IT'S BETTER TO DO IT AND BE TERRIFIED THAN NOT DO IT AND BE TERRIFIED.

I heard this quote for the first time at a masterclass taught by the songwriter Shoshana Bean (at least, I think it was her, I had been day drinking) in 2010, when I was at the Edinburgh Fringe Festival. If you haven't been to Edinburgh and you love comedy, theatre and drinking—please, drop what you are doing right now and book a ticket. You *have* to go. The festival's like Mecca for theatre and comedy, with a mix of new performers and huge-name performers. There's literally theatre and comedy 24/7 for nearly a month. Any and every space in the town is used as a makeshift theatre. The uni, parks, people's houses

(that they live in!), restaurants and cafés become perform-
ance spaces. It's crazy. If you didn't like theatre and lived in
Edinburgh, you'd have to leave town for a month. It's amazing
and manic and, obviously, I love it.

I've been to Edinburgh twice. The first time was to stage-
manage a theatre venue and the second time was to 'produce'
a show with my friend. We phoned it in *hard*. I still feel bad
about what a crap job we did, to be honest. We were terrible
producers of that show. I mean this: *never* hire us. We literally did nothing. Well, actually, that's not strictly true. We
did see a lot of other shows and eat a fair amount of deep-
fried Mars Bars.

One of the best things about the festival is the masterclasses:
basically, lectures by people in comedy or theatre who have
lessons to impart to young, naïve wannabes like me. I was at
a time in my life where I felt like something was going to shift
for me—I was just waiting to see what it would be.

At Shoshana's masterclass, I was furiously writing everything
down because I was so inspired by her enthusiasm. I felt like
she was talking only to me.

'It's better to do it and be terrified than not do it and be
terrified,' she said. I wrote it down, and then wrote over the
words again and again, so they stood out. Something clicked.
I was 25 years old and all I wanted to do was stand-up. *It's
better to do it and be terrified than not do it and be terrified.*

So, two nights later, after years of wanting to and being too
afraid, I stood up at a microphone with that quote in my head.
It was midnight, and I was in a shitty bar at a shitty open mic
night. I was drunk and my act was heavily improvised, but I

fucking did it. I did stand-up. For seven minutes, I stood on that stage and, for about 10 seconds of those seven minutes, I made people laugh. I did it. I fucking did it.

It was elation, the highest of highs. I had overcome my greatest fear.

The liberation of that moment informed so much of my career. These days, before I do anything, I think about what Shoshana said: *It's better to do it and be terrified than not do it and be terrified.*

The thing is, I don't want to look back on my life and think: *Why didn't I do that? I always wanted to do that. Why did I hold myself back?* I don't want to regret anything. And since 2010, I haven't.

(Fun fact: In my early videos, this quote is on the wall behind me.)

SOME MORE QUOTES TO LIVE BY

Here are some other quotes I feel are worthy of your vision boards. Some are anonymous, some are from famous people, and some are just amazing quotes I had to include.

Work hard so your heroes become your rivals.

No day but today. (Jonathan Larson)

Having a soft heart in a cruel world is courage, not weakness. (Katherine Henson)

You can have results or excuses, not both. (Arnold Schwarzenegger)

Go instead where there is no path and leave a trail. (Ralph Waldo Emerson)

Wanting to be someone else is a waste of who you are. (Kurt Cobain)

Be yourself; everyone else is already taken. (Oscar Wilde)

Never make permanent decisions on temporary feelings.

Picasso said he would paint with his own wet tongue on the dusty floor of a jail cell if he had to. We have to create; it is the only thing louder than destruction. (Andrea Gibson)

R

R

IS FOR . . .

RADIO

I think people have this idea that radio is really glamorous and easy and fun. And, to be honest, it is a really good job. Sitting and talking with no make-up on? I mean . . . that's for me.

But everyone thinks that it's as simple as having a conversation with your mate, and playing some songs. Here are some radio realities . . .

- Starting work at 4 a.m.—day after day—is fucking hard. Like *so hard*. People say that it's like anything else and you 'get used to it' but you don't. Ever. I once worked with an announcer who was in his 70s. He'd been doing breakfast

189

radio for 50 years, and I asked him for some advice. He said, 'Well, here's the thing. You'll never—ever—get used to the hours. So, the best thing to do is just to accept that now.'

- Breakfast radio finishes at 9 a.m., but that doesn't mean you do. We work till at least 9.15.
- If you work in a content shift, your brain never turns off. Everything you do, watch, talk about, see and consume becomes content. I have been known to do some dumb stuff just for content. Like the time I helped castrate a cow. Long story.
- Your friends hate you because every conversation you have with them becomes fodder for the show. Eventually, they'll start saying things like, 'Now, before I tell you this, you can't say this on the radio.'
- They'll also hate you because they'll be telling you a really sad story and, instead of saying, 'Oh my god, I'm sorry,' you say, 'That's a great phone topic. 13 10 60, call us if your husband has cheated on you with four women.'
- Announcers don't choose the music.
- When you're on air, you never really hear the ads or music, though, because you're prepping (aka watching videos on your phone).
- Most people in breakfast radio gain at least five kilos because of the weird hours and the fact that you're drinking heaps of coffee, and croissants go really well with coffee, etc, etc. I gained 25 because I'm competitive.
- Fact: headphones make your hair super greasy.

- We genuinely love it when people call and tell us amazing stories. Call us.

- We also genuinely love giving away prizes. It's like being Oprah.

- Speaking of prizes, we think long and hard about what to give away. And for every radio comp that makes it on air, you can bet there are at least 10 to 15 ideas that didn't get up. Once, my co-announcer was desperate to do a promo called 'Trip or Snip': if you won, you got a holiday in Thailand. The loser got a free vasectomy. Nobody really went for it, though. Sad.

- Radio announcers run at a delay all the time because sh*t f*cking happens. Normally, it's seven to 30 seconds.

- Your relationship with your co-host is complicated, to say the least. Usually, you spend in excess of 70 hours together a week. That's more than most people spend with their partners. On top of that, you call, email and text each other when you're *not* together. And it's not like a normal working relationship—when you have disagreements, you can't just storm out and leave. When the song ends and you're back on air, you have to sound like you're best buddies again. You're stuck in a small room together for five, and sometimes six, days a week, starting at 4.15 a.m. It can be . . . full on, but the pressure can lead to an amazing friendship.

- Radio ratings days are either amazing or harrowing. Either way, you get free drinks.

- Interviewing celebrities isn't always fun.

REAL BAD BOYS

My boyfriend, Tom, thinks he's a bad boy. This is Tom.

Tom is *not* a bad boy. The guy calls himself a bad boy. Once you call yourself a bad boy, you're probably/definitely not one.

Actually, he's about the furthest thing from a bad boy you'll ever meet.

For example:

- When we fly, Tom keeps his seatbelt on at all times. Even when the seatbelt sign is turned off.
- He never jaywalks. Not even when there are no other cars. 'Wait for the green light, Tanya.'

- He drives like a nana. 'Better to get there safely than not at all, Tanya.'
- Unlike most 25-year-old men, he watches baby animals, not porn, for hours on YouTube. (I'm sure he also watches porn, just not when I'm around.)
- He opens car doors for people. I mean . . . this guy is delusional if he thinks that he's a bad boy.
- One time, when an old man was locked out of his house, Tom got a locksmith to go there, and then paid for it.
- Tom has turned down club nights to babysit his sister's kids.
- He asked to watch *The Notebook* the other day and said, 'Ryan Gosling shines in this role.'
- His Spotify playlist has Miley Cyrus's 'The Climb' and 'Hoedown Throwdown' on it.

Yeah . . . you're a real bad boy, mate.

ROMANCE

I'm sending my boyfriend to TAFE to learn how to be more romantic. Is there a course in that?

Tom is great, but like many boys he's just—how shall I say this?—completely crap with feelings. He finds it so hard to communicate how he feels, which is really frustrating because I'm really good at it (#arrogant). I feel like I have so many feelings (ALL THE FEELINGS) about him, and I tell him all the time and I just want, even once, for him to articulate how he feels about me.

Here's a sample of some of our most recent texts:

Me: *You are the cutest boy. I'm obsessed with you.*
Tom: *Hey, I start work at 12.*

Me: *I wish you were here with me, I miss the way you smell.*
Tom: *OK. My phone is about to die.*

Me: *You're my favourite person.*
Tom: *doesn't reply*

Me: *You make my life so much better.*
Tom: *doesn't reply*

Me: *You make the hard simple.*
Tom: *doesn't reply*

Me: *You are the sun in the rain.*
Tom: *doesn't reply*

Me: *I love you.*
Tom: *OK. I'm with Jarrod.*

RAUNCHY

When Tom and I were in a long-distance relationship, we would only get to see each other once a month or so. It was always exciting and fun, though, and, yep, it made for some pretty hot bedroom times.

Hahahahhaaa LOL. Jokes. Imagine.

A few years back, Tom meets me at the airport. He hands me food because he knows I'll be starving (it was a one-hour

Jetstar flight; cheese and biscuits were $19) and, immediately, I know something is up. He's wearing nice clothes (usually he picks me up in trackies) and has this aftershave on that I love.

Oh god, I think. *He wants sexy times.*

With every passing moment, I feel more and more guilty because, right now, I look like the complete opposite of a sexy time. My hair is all over the place and littered with greys. I haven't shaved my legs or underarms or, indeed, any part of my body in . . . let's just call it a very long time. I'm not wearing any make-up, as always. Tom takes my bags and flashes me this big smile.

Oh Jesus.

We get to the hotel, and I realise I haven't brought any underwear that's not beige and baggy. I look around in my bag, hoping to find the one Victoria's Secret nightie I own, but instead find my loose pyjama top emblazoned with *Donut Judge Me*. It was once white but I've owned it for so long, it's off grey, the fabric is thinning in parts and has a rip in it.

As I get into bed, where Tom is lying, practically with a rose between his teeth, he looks at me and I say, sheepishly, 'I'm sorry.'

He shakes his head like, *No, it's cool*, and I think: *Okay, go in for a pash. Save the day, Hennessy.* So I go in for a smooch and Tom recoils.

'Tanya, when was the last time you brushed your teeth?'

I think for a moment. Which is apparently a bit too long.

'Tanya!'

'Mate. This is who I am. Donut judge me.'

S

S IS FOR...

SINGLE

Have you ever been a third wheel? You know, a single person hanging out with a couple.

Worst ever.

No. Wait. Sorry. The *worst* worst ever is being a fifth wheel: a single person with *two* couples. Excruciating.

I was single for seven years, so when I was single, I was the Singlest Single to Ever Be Single. And—just my luck—I hung out with couples all the time.

Sometimes being the third or fifth wheel is weird and awkward for you, the single person, but sometimes it's weird for the couple. Like the time I went to my friend's wedding in Fiji and the only people I knew were her and her husband. So I hung out with them on their honeymoon.

I didn't even realise what I was doing. I saw them at the pool because it was at a resort and then I just . . . didn't leave them. Even when they said they were going back to their room, I didn't get the hint.

'Sure,' I said. 'Sounds good. Room service! I want a burger.'

It wasn't until my friend awkwardly shut the door on me that I realised they wanted me out. (I ended up just sitting near the entrance to their room, in case they wanted to come get dinner later.)

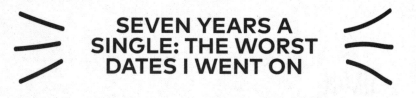

SEVEN YEARS A SINGLE: THE WORST DATES I WENT ON

- The guy who ate food off my plate and told me I was 'zany'. Somehow, I agreed to a second date with this guy and he . . . brought along a test for me to do. Like, a printed-off test (background: he was a teacher). At dinner, he tested me on my geography knowledge and, after an embarrassingly low number of correct answers, he told me he was 'getting his red pen out'. It wasn't even a euphemism.

- The guy who said: 'Please, put your wallet away—I'm paying. It's actually so nice to have money now; when I

was working in London I was getting paid in cocaine and I never had any cash, so, really, it's my treat.'
- The guy who wore no shoes, and tracksuit pants he had cut off to make shorts (tracksuit shorts, I guess?).
- The guy who had 'FUCK' tattooed on his torso. I wish I was joking.

OH, AND THE ONE BAD DATE I DIDN'T HAVE

We once ran a comp on air to find me a boyfriend (so fun!). We did this thing called 'Dating in the Dark', where a bunch of guys and I would talk and I'd choose someone based on their personality. I chose this guy who seemed really funny and nice and (honestly, most importantly) normal.

The next day, on air, we find out he's hot AF and, secretly, I'm thanking my lucky stars that my co-announcer was so sick of me whingeing about being single that he came up with this competition.

We sent the lucky dude a $100 voucher for a local restaurant, and my phone number. He never called.

On second thoughts, I should have taken the voucher to the restaurant.

On third thoughts, I shouldn't have let the station run a competition to find me a boyfriend.

WHAT NOT TO SAY TO A SINGLE GIRL

'Don't worry, you'll find someone someday.'
What day? When? What time? What do they look like? TELL ME.

'Just don't turn into some crazy cat lady.'
Soz. Too late.

'I don't know why you're single! You're such a catch! What's wrong with the men out there?'
Totally agree.

(*At a wedding*) 'You'd better get out there, they're doing the bouquet toss.'
I know they are. I am aware because 50 other people have said that exact thing to me in the last 10 minutes.

'It'll happen when you least expect it.'
I have not been 'expecting it' for the last four years.

'You have to love yourself before you can love someone else.'
Ugh.

'Is it hard, because you thought you would be married by now?'
Yes . . . thank you for bringing up what I cry about alone.

'You're too picky.'
No, *you're* too talky.

'Have you thought about dating online?'
You're the first person to ever suggest that . . . *eye roll*

'Do you think you focus too much on your career?'
Probably. Yes.

'I couldn't imagine being single. You poor thing.'
Farrrrking hell, this is rude.

'We'll all be laughing about this someday.'
Which day?

'You need to go out more.'
Going out is the worst. Hard pass.

'What was wrong with that last guy?'
He liked Nickelback.

'One day, when you're married, you'll wish you were single.'
UGGGHHHHHHHH, SHUT UP.

HOW TO
STAY SINGLE

I was single for seven years (I'm not sure if I've mentioned this yet, but there it is) so I know *a lot* about being single . . . and staying that way. If you've ever wanted to stay single for an uncomfortable amount of time, here's what you do (trust me, many of these worked for me):

- If you have the option of a *Dance Moms* marathon or going to a party with lots of single men, it's Abby Lee *errrytime*.
- When you do meet a single guy, make sure you tell him how undesired you are by other men.
- Always appear tired and dishevelled. Cannot overstate the importance of this.
- Mention how desperate you are. Constantly.
- Talk about children straight up. For example: 'I'm running out of eggs. I want children. Three. In three years.'
- Always have a knife on your person. It makes you look hot and also super rational.
- Go back 290 weeks in their Insta and double-tap a single pic.
- Ask your date how much money they make BEFORE you ask their name.
- Deal with your major issues on dates. Treat your date like a free therapist.
- Invest in super-hot friends. This way, no men will ever even notice you. Believe me, it works.
- If you notice a dark boob hair, show it to any guy you meet. Men are interested in that kind of thing.

BEING SINGLE AT WEDDINGS

Weddings are fun because you get a free meal and all the booze and, usually, a good cake (unless it's one of those hipster weddings where they serve a wheel of cheese instead of real cake. Cheese is not cake. Don't force it. It's just not. Serve a vanilla sponge or a red velvet, and call it a day).

Anyway. Weddings are fun.

But when you're single, weddings can be . . . less fun? More . . . torture.

Destination weddings when you're single are a particular type of hell. At my friend's wedding in Fiji, I felt like I was the only single person on the whole bloody island. There were couples everywhere, pashing on hammocks, laughing in the pool and lighting wish lanterns. The wedding was amazing, and I had fun, but the end of the reception was a real defining point for me.

As per bridal tradition, it came to the point in the night when the bride throws her bouquet over her shoulder. I was the MC, so I called the single ladies to the dance floor to catch it. I quickly realised that there was no one on the dance floor . . . but me. I was the only single at the wedding. Huh. So, the bride awkwardly handed me the bouquet.

Handed me the bouquet.

Sorry, just so we are clear.

She walked over and HANDED ME THE BOUQUET.

IN FRONT OF EVERYONE AT THE WEDDING.

I laughed, because if I hadn't, I would have cried.

As I was walking back to my room after the reception, an elderly man came up to me and said: 'Young lady, I had to wait until I was 45 to find my wife. It's better to be in the right relationship than just any relationship. You want to be with someone who is perfect for you? Well, you might just have to wait, like I did.'

He was right, of course.

But he also wasn't the one who was *handed a fucking bouquet.*

SINGLE AND DATING

When you're single for seven years, you do a fair bit of online dating. And, after a while, Tinder and eHarmony and whatever don't cut it. You just see the same old guys over and over and over. So I went in search of something different. *Someone* different. Here are the five most obscure dating websites I've actually looked at to try to find a guy.

Clowndating.com The website said: 'Let a clown love you. This site is for dating carnies and circus folk.' If you have a spare 20 minutes at work, get on this site.

Wealthymen.com Such a great way to start a relationship: on the proviso that he makes over $85K.

Mulletpassions.com You must have a mullet. You must love a mullet.

Glutenfreesingles.com This, SERIOUSLY, is what the site says: 'A dating network where you never have to feel alone, awkward, or a burden because you are gluten free.' . . . Are they kidding with this? Pretty much everyone is gluten free, or at least off carbs, now.

Mimepassions.com This kills me: 'A 100% free social networking & online dating site specifically for singles with a passion for Mime (and for Mimes). Sign up now to enjoy free Mime chat. Please note that we ask that no one speak out loud within the Mime chatroom, out of respect for the art form.' I mean . . . mic drop. That is the best this book is gunna get (and I didn't even write it).

STALKER

Ever been prank called?

Ever been prank called multiple times at midnight, with the person saying your full name and your address, the day after you've moved into your new apartment?

In January 2017 I moved into a new apartment in Canberra with Tom. It was only down the road, literally a five-minute walk, from the old place. But we had a fridge, washing machine, big couches and a bed, and it was summer and we didn't wanna sweat, so we hired a removalist company.

We could have done it ourselves and saved some money. But moving is hell and I was like, 'Take my money, I'm so lazy.'

So, we moved in with the help of two young guys and we were set. In saying that, one of them broke a light fitting in our bedroom. Ugh.

It was a Sunday and because I was doing brekky radio, Tom and I were in bed at 9 p.m. As it was January, it was hot as balls, like 44 degrees . . . we had no air-con, the fans were going but nothing was cooling us down. It was hard to get to sleep.

But it was about to get even harder.

It would have been around 10 p.m. when my phone rang. It was an unknown number.

I answered . . . not really thinking. I guess I thought maybe it was my co-announcer trying to prank me for the show the next day, or Optus telling me to pay my phone bill, which I'd been putting off for months.

'Hey, it's Tanya.'

I heard a male voice. He laughed, then a female voice joined in with the laughing.

They hung up.

Thirty seconds later, there was another call from the unknown number. (I now know an unknown number means the person is calling using the internet, so there's a fun fact. #thisbookiseducational) It was the same thing: breathing and laughing. I kept asking, 'Who is this? Hello?' and they just laughed for what seemed like two minutes. I hung up.

By this time, Tom had woken up. I was feeling stressed out by the eeriness of these people calling, laughing and hanging up, late at night.

Tom told me it was probably my co-announcer and his girlfriend, and I agreed.

The phone rang again, so painfully loud. We were still in darkness. I was freaking out now.

I didn't pick up; it went to voicemail and to text. The text I got read: *Tanya Hennessy, 41 ********* Street Crace.*

I felt sick. *Did someone just watch us move in? How'd they get my number? Are they watching us now? Can they see us?*

I didn't sleep well that whole night. I imagined someone was under the bed, or watching us, or waiting for us to leave the building so they could kill us. Yes I know. Irrational.

But that's me.

I went to work at 4 a.m. I was a zombie.

When the show was finished, we called the police. Because I work in the public eye and had been threatened before, online, they took it seriously, and said they would trace the call and find out who it was, and drive around the street at night.

I couldn't leave work, I didn't want to be in the apartment alone. For a whole week, I waited from 1 p.m. till 5 p.m. at the station for Tom to finish work.

We got a baseball bat and hid it under the bed, because the phone rang again on Tuesday, and they laughed and hung up. It was so scary. I felt so on edge.

The police kept calling to make sure I was okay and nothing new had happened, which was amazing of them. I turned off all my social media where my locations could be found, hid any videos that showed whereabouts I lived. I went into hyper-drive security. I made Tom walk me to my car every morning because I was so terrified.

Friday, the police called. 'Tanya, do you know a ********
****** [insert name here]?'

'No,' I said. 'I don't know who that is. Never heard of them.'

'He was the man who moved you into your house. One of the removalists. He's only 22 and he told us he used your information to call you using the internet. We went to his house, and he said he did it because he wanted to scare you, so you would talk about it on air. He just wanted to be mentioned on the radio. Do you want to press charges?'

'That little shit! No, I don't. Tell him never, ever to do that to me or anyone ever again.'

(This is paraphrased, by the way . . .)

It was the bloody removalist.

But I kinda felt like I got the last laugh, because even though all he wanted was to be talked about on air, he never got what he wanted.

But, then again, maybe he got the last laugh—because he's now in a book.

It also turns out he was the one who broke the light fitting, which resulted in us having to pay $100 out of our bond to get it replaced. Fucker.

T
IS FOR...

TIME

Over time, things in relationships change. They just do, no matter how hard you try or how much you want to 'keep things fresh'. It's best when you have given up and don't care about being domestically nude together, but you do miss that initial giddy feeling you had for each other.

Anyway, there's a big difference between your relationship after two weeks . . . and two years. For instance:

Grooming
Two weeks: Tan, heels, make-up every day.
Two years: Trackies, no bra, visible pimple cream.

Texting

Two weeks: *Wanna come over for dinner? Xxxxxx I will make you something amazing.*

Two years: *On way home. Heading to shops. Will get tacos and toilet paper. Also you didn't put down the toilet seat, you dick.*

Bodily functions

Two weeks: You don't have any.

Two years: Open-bathroom-door policy.

Body grooming

Two weeks: Like a hairless cat.

Two years: 'Babe, look at this pimple I have on my bum.'

Dates

Two weeks: Flirting over cocktails, and going to the movies and finding your hands in the popcorn bucket at the same time.

Two years: Cereal in a bowl on the couch; no talking.

Sleeping

Two weeks: Spooning.

Two years: 'Don't touch me. You're in your area and I'm in mine.'

Sex

Two weeks: All the time. Every day. Multiple times a day.

Two years: As long as it fits in around *Game of Thrones*.

TURKEY

I love Turkey. Both the bird and the country. But I haven't eaten Turkish cuisine since I went to Turkey (country, not bird) with my friend Lydia a few years back.

Lydia and I went backpacking across Europe for six months. And we decided to eat our way through Europe. Our love of food is so great that, to be honest, we went to Turkey basically because we wanted to have a real Turkish mezze plate. You know, a platter filled with dolmades, feta and various Mediterranean finger foods, along with lots of dips and bread. All the good stuff.

So, when we arrived in Antalya, on the Turkish coast, we set out on an epic adventure to find the best, most authentic Turkish mezze plate we could.

We wanted to find somewhere authentic; the kind of place that was run by a family and handed down through the generations. After a bit of searching, we found somewhere called Authentic Turkish Restaurant. Bingo.

The place smelled incredible, and it had a stunning view of some ocean I should know the name of and don't, so we were *in*. We proudly ordered our magical mezze plate, and watched as the feast unfolded before us. Dolmades, sliced meats, eggplant salad, lamb kofta, feta cheese, hummus and, of course, Turkish bread. Heaven.

There were also some things on the plate we didn't recognise, but we were overseas, and when you're overseas you're like: 'I'm overseas! I'm a traveller! I'll put anything in my mouth!' So, we went to town.

The best part of the mezze plate was this truly amazing white dip. It was delicious. So moreish. I'd never had anything like it. We ate the entire ramekin of it and asked for another two! And we ate those too—no drama—with a spoon. With a *spoon,* I tell you! It was that good.

Three hours later, we asked the owner about the dip. What was *in* it? How did they get it to taste so good? Again, I don't really cook, like, as a general life rule, but I was prepared to break that rule to make this dip at home.

'Not dip,' he said, with a thick accent.

'Yeah, it was!' we protested. 'The white dip we ate with a spoon . . . that dip.'

'Not dip. It is . . . how you say? Butter.'

What now?

'Butter.'

Butter.

We (mainly me) had eaten three ramekins (with a *spoon*, no less) of BUTTER.

Yeah. I'm not proud of it.

But, to my and Lydia's credit, it was the best brand of butter you can buy in Turkey.

TRAVELLING

Travelling is always fun, but travelling in your 20s is way different from travelling in your 30s.

Destination

20s: Ibiza.

30s: Wherever smarttraveller.gov.au says is currently safe.

Packing

20s: 'Fuck it, basics only!'

30s: 'Everything must be compartmentalised! Do you have the sunscreen? Do we have enough hand sanitiser? Make sure everything in your carry-on is in zip-lock bags!'

Accommodation

20s: 'I'll sort it out when I get there. I'll sleep at the airport if I have to.'

30s: 'If it's not five-star, I'm not leaving the country.'

Food

20s: 'I'm a worldly traveller. I eat everything. Besides, lizard sperm is amazing when it's cooked right!'

30s: 'Is this lactose free? Do you have lactose free? Can you drink the water here? Is the ice made with clean water? What are the vegan options?'

Sightseeing

20s: 'Paris really comes alive at night, anyway. We don't need to go anywhere today.' (*Sleeps off hangover for 13 hours*)

30s: 'Let's get up at 4 a.m. and see the sunrise and the temples.'

Airline

20s: 'Jetstar is fine.'

30s: 'Jetstar is fine.'

 # A LIST OF THINGS THAT WILL HAPPEN IF YOU'RE TRAVELLING WITH YOUR MOTHER

- 🍫 She will complain that New York is 'too loud'.
- 🍫 She will snore if you share a room.
- 🍫 She will buy terrible souvenirs (e.g. a plate with her face on it).

- She will wear an embarrassingly large hat and visible sunscreen.
- She will take such awful photos of you that you have to awkwardly ask a stranger to take your pic and then pose alone (because: Instagram).
- She will book strange things, like a Fourth of July Over 50s Cruise. For the two of you.
- You will spend a lot of time looking at 'slacks' and sensible walking sandals while shopping.
- She will cry a lot and say things like, 'I just love spending this time with you.'
- She will get so excited when she meets another Aussie overseas.
- You will never enter a bar or club—even if she wants to, you just can't be seen with your mum in a New York club. (God, who am I kidding? I don't want to be in a club either. Actually, it's kind of convenient travelling with your mum because you always have an excuse to be in bed by 10 p.m. If you were with friends or a partner, you'd feel bad about going to bed early, but with your mum, you're like, *She's old, I don't want her roaming the streets alone; I'd better go with her.*)

U

IS FOR . . .

UMMMMMM (OR IS IT OMMMMMM?)

I really want to be someone who can meditate. I have been to some classes and I have the apps but I just can't do it.

They say, 'Clear your mind and relax,' and it's like my brain goes, 'Think every thought you have ever had and tense, bitch.'

It just doesn't work for me. I'm too much of a stressy anxious mess to do it. (Which is exactly *why* I *need* to do it.)

Here are some thoughts I have had while attempting to meditate:

- *How long into this am I?*
- *I'm bored.*

- *You're doing this, you're actually doing something you said you would do.*
- *What time is it?*
- *What should I have for dinner?*
- *Am I doing this right?*
- *I'm so zen, I can't wait to tell people I meditate now.*
- *This guy's voice is weird. Is he British or just pretentious?*
- *I'm gunna do this every day.*
- *My back hurts.*
- *This is the worst. I never want to do this again.*
- *Is this how I breathe?*
- *Am I breathing properly?*
- *I have forgotten how to breathe.*
- *Is this how you breathe?*
- *Ah, now I have time to think about and relive and over-analyse all the awkward things I did today.*
- *I think I want Subway for dinner.*
- *I think they have changed their cookie recipe.*
- *I miss Pizza Hut.*
- *The Pizza Hut you could dine in and it was a buffet of pizza.*
- *Oh, they had a dessert bar there too!*
- *How good is jelly?*
- *I haven't had jelly in ages.*
- *I wonder what my boss thinks of me?*
- *Should I get a fringe?*
- *I want to get teeth whitening.*
- *Have I done this long enough?*
- *Ah, I'm one minute and 13 seconds in.*

V
IS FOR...

VIRAL

If you have ever experienced bullying in your life, you'll know how truly horrendous it feels. It's awful.

Bullying feels like that voice inside your head—the one that tells you that you're crap, that you're not funny and that you're a fraud—but from someone else. It's like it confirms every single word of negative self-talk you've ever thought. It's a scary place to be.

Being bullied online was one of the lowest points of my life.

About a year after I got my job in Canberra, I was at my parents' house in Newcastle, trying to get the URL to my Facebook page to send to some website. I typed my name into the search field, and the second result after my official page was one called THE TANYA HENNESSY CAMPAIGN TO HAVE HER REMOVED FROM HIT104.7.

(That title doesn't even make sense.)

I felt sick. The pit of my stomach dropped. I immediately started to cry. Not sobbing—just single tears that slowly rolled into my mouth.

The group had 125 members, and I couldn't help but click through to see what people had said. I shouldn't have, because as I began scrolling the hate comments were gut-wrenching.

I felt sick reading them. I almost couldn't believe it. Had I done anything that bad to deserve these comments?

I do want to say, of course people are entitled to an opinion. If I'm not your cup of tea, that's fine. We all like different stuff. But there is a difference between that opinion and what I was reading, which was mean, cold and plain disgusting.

I looked at who the members were. These people lived in the same town as me. I recognised some of their workplaces. Some of them had friends who were also my friends.

I kept staring at the screen, salty tears rolling into my mouth.

I remembered when I'd taken the job, only a few months before, saying—half-jokingly—that the worst thing that could happen if I took the job was someone starting a hate page dedicated to me.

And now they had.

As I stared and scrolled, I noticed the page had been started on 8 September 2016. I stopped in my tracks. I felt sick. The date stood out for me and I quickly realised why: it was R U OK? Day, a day promoting mental health awareness and suicide prevention.

Someone had started this page the same day I'd talked on radio about how much I had been bullied online. I'd spoken openly and honestly about how online bullies had put me into a state of significant depression.

Earlier that year, I'd had online trolls tell me I should have been aborted. People wrote in saying that they wanted to kill themselves, our show was so bad.

It was a sad and lonely time. I used to cry and cry and cry every day when I finished work. Sometimes I would just lie under my bed. I just felt so alone and scared. I felt so anxious about going on air because every time I said something—literally anything—I was giving the trolls more fodder.

On air on R U OK? Day, I wanted to share the reality of what had happened. I wanted people to know they were not alone if they had been bullied or suffered from anxiety or depression. I wanted people to know that if they were struggling they should reach out for help, or if they thought someone else was struggling, reach out to them.

I also wanted bullies to know how just how much effect their comments on the internet could have on an individual. I think a lot of people believe their words don't mean anything online and that they don't affect people.

Here's what I said on air.

I have been deaf.

I'm starting to hear now . . . but for a really long time I was deaf.

I couldn't hear positives. I couldn't hear anything good. Because when we moved to this station in Canberra in January, Ryan (my co-announcer) and I were mercilessly bullied online. It took a massive toll on my life, my mental health and my confidence.

We took over from a well-loved show and it was tough. Like, really tough. People were so passionate about the show we took over from.

The things people were saying about us even before we were on air was awful . . . getting online at that time was horrific. Even if I was offline people would send me text messages with screenshots of things people had said about me/us.

I moved here alone, I left my boyfriend in Queensland. My family is five hours away.

I was painfully alone. And people were just raining down hate at every turn.

Here are some of the comments so you get the idea . . .

This is why women shouldn't be on the radio.

She is an embarrassment to women.

Ryan and Tanya are the worst thing to happen to Canberra.

She's so unfunny and she thinks she's funny. She's painful. Get her off the air.

Plz Tanya Fuck off from the radio. I swear you are the shittest radio announcer I have ever heard and believe me every person I work with and that I have spoken too agrees. Do Canberra a favour and go find another job. I have heard autistic kids make more sense than what you dribble in the mornings. You sound like an idiot every morning

I feel sorry for this girl's boyfriend. She's an embarrassment

This woman is the stupidest woman alive. She is awful. Fucking dumb bitch. Someone fire her.

I wish she had been aborted.

This chick gives me cancer.

On air, I shared that I was struggling to find new friends. I was bullied for saying I was struggling.

Someone wrote, *You deserve to have no friends. You're disgusting.*

Apart from finding new friends, I was doing new things, so I did a dance class. I'm not a dancer. I was completely out of my comfort zone. So vulnerable. But I went along, and at the end I did a Facebook video post about how liberated I felt to find some new friends and how proud I was of myself for going to this dance class.

Then I saw a comment on Facebook which was my tipping point. It said, *This woman is so annoying. I want to hit this woman over the head with a chair.* That same person then also inboxed to my page, *The things that I want to do to you are so brutal, I can't even write them down.*

It killed me. It made me want to disappear. I wanted to crash my car so I didn't have to be here anymore.

I didn't want to go anywhere in case someone who had threatened me actually made good with their threat.

I was crying most days.

I needed my family and friends to ask if I was okay.

I needed my boyfriend to have conversations with me.

I needed to talk it through.

I needed them to reach out.

I needed to talk.

My mum and dad were here a lot. I needed them.

Without my mum and my boyfriend, I don't know if I would still be in this job. Or be here at all.

I needed someone to ask if I was okay. Because I really wasn't.

Right now, I'm fine. I have come through it.

I have come out of it better. Stronger. I now have procedures and ways to deal with the hate online and the spiralling of anxiety and depression.

Know that a simple conversation, human interaction and compassion can help people from making a serious life-or-death decision.

Through connection and asking one question, you can save a life . . . and that is what R U OK? Day is about.

I was deaf and the only question I could hear was— are you okay?

I'm so thankful that I was asked.

We get so busy and caught up in our lives that we forget to ask.

But we have to make time in our days.

We need to reach out. You are not alone.

Today, and every day, if someone doesn't seem themself, even if they do. Smiles don't mean people are okay. Find the right time and ask: are you okay?

So, to recap: the very same day I talked about trolling and how much it had affected my mental health, some guy started a page to get me fired.

I mean . . . kick me when I'm down.

Who would bully someone for being honest and starting an important conversation about mental health?

Who would start a page dedicated to hating someone, knowing they suffered from depression as a result of online bullying?

Who would join that page?

It took weeks, but Facebook finally took the page down.

Thank god.

I should say I had a lot of support at this time too. A lot of people defended me and supported me. So many people reached out to me and shared their stories with me. To those people, I am forever indebted to you. You were the sunshine in the rain.

I'm so glad I got through it. Because there was a while where I didn't think I could or would. I thought I was going to go under. But I didn't and I'm so thankful I didn't.

Every year in Australia we lose eight lives a day to suicide. Suicide is the leading cause of death for 18- to 25-year-olds. This is terrifying. This year alone we have lost so many children and young adults from online (and offline) bullying. This is an epidemic. It is so very serious. I know how serious it is because of my own experience. Something needs to change.

If you are going through anything like this, my advice is to reach out and talk about what's going on. Tell your family and friends how you are feeling. Talk about it and be really honest. A problem shared is a problem halved. Go outside, go to the beach or the park. Walk. Definitely seek professional advice (from counsellors or psychologists) and be kind to yourself. Surround yourself with your biggest cheerleaders and know that you are not alone.

Speak, even if your voice shakes.

If you or anyone you know is struggling or needs help, please contact Lifeline on 13 11 14 or beyondblue on 1300 22 4636.

 # WHAT ACTUALLY HAPPENS WHEN YOUR VIDEO GOES VIRAL

I'm lucky enough to have made a few videos that have had millions of views and gone viral. My 'Realistic Make-Up Tutorial' video has been seen by 250 million people. I know. Mental, right? I'm still jaw-to-the-floor shocked that so many people would watch something I filmed on an iPhone I'd gaffer-taped to a pole.

My first video was 'The Difference Between 18 and 30'. I got 1.3 million views in 24 hours. I went from 2000 Facebook followers to 25,000.

I kept refreshing to check if the numbers were right. It just didn't seem like they could be. How could the number of views be going up so fast? It didn't make any sense.

Here's what I've learned about what happens when your video goes viral.

- Your phone explodes. My phone had so many notifications, I had to turn them off.
- A lot of your high school 'mates' remember how much they liked you and add you on Facebook.
- People want to buy your page. I got an offer of $240 and one camel. (I didn't take it. I'm holding out for two camels, so they can be friends.)
- People want you to spruik their stuff. Teeth-whitening products, make-up, clothing, skinny tea, what have you.
- Charities approach you. *Can you please post about my charity dog wash in Louisiana, Tina? Sure,* I write back. *It's Tanya, and I live in Australia, but sure.*
- People yell stuff at you from their cars. Like:
  'Are you that girl who does those videos?'
  'Are you internet famous?'
  'I don't find you funny. Can I have a photo for my Snapchat?'
  'I don't know your name. Can I have a photo?'
  'You're shorter than I thought you'd be.'
- People ask you things like, 'How do you do it?' and 'How do you make something go viral?' And the answer is, you can't. You can't *make* something go viral. My videos were flukes, that's the truth of it, and I think most super-successful videos and memes are. Seriously, the day I released the video 'Things People Say to Make-up Artists', I had just had a conversation with my friend Ellie (who is a make-up artist) about the shit people must say to her. When she

started telling me about it, I was like, 'Oh, I have to make a video!' I shot the video that day on my iPhone and edited it with iMovie (also on my phone) on a plane later that night, in under 50 minutes. In fact, I learned to edit *on the plane*. See? Actual fluke.

- You will *love it*. Well, I do, anyway. It's amazing! The best part of doing video content is that real live actual people who are time poor have actively given up their time to watch what you've created. It's the coolest thing to realise that your stuff is being shared because people like it. It makes up for bullying comments.

W

IS FOR . . .

WORKAHOLIC

I have another addiction. An obsession, even. It's not healthy. I thought it was for a long while, but as time goes on, I realise it's not.

I'm addicted to work. Obsessed with work.

I know this because I have a one-hour flight and, instead of 'wasting it' doing nothing, I'm writing this after a 15-hour day.

I know I'm not alone in this. Thanks to social media and the internet being on phones, the separation between work and life is harder.

When my mother was my age, she was either at work or at home. When she went on holidays, she was on holidays and no one expected her to work. Nowadays, that just isn't the case. Work is omnipresent. Everyone is on a device. With work emails, we have become 'available' 24/7. This leads to anxiety, depression and burnout. The simple solution? Just turn off your phone, or don't answer work emails after hours.

Ha. Imagine.

I mean, look . . . you could—but it's almost gotten to a point where that isn't a thing anymore. Especially if you're a millennial.

It's a dog-eat-dog world—so if you wanna get ahead in your career, 24/7 availability is what you do. You answer your work emails on toilets while at a wedding reception or birthday party.

It's hard to do otherwise when you're passionate about what you do. When you really love your work, it makes it easier to prioritise it above everything else.

It obviously differs depending on your age, job and where you are in your life, of course. I know that for a lot of my friends who are media professionals, switching off is just not an option. Especially if they have a job that involves the 24-hour news cycle and social media. It's a part of the hustle now.

I genuinely do worry for us. Because it's no real way to live. I live like this and it's exhausting but I don't know how to rewire my brain.

One of my biggest issues is that I'm addicted to work and I can't figure out how to work less. It's a First World problem, no doubt, but it's still very real.

I am stuck in a strange place where I work in order to reduce guilt. I feel guilt if I don't work. The guilt is painful. So, I work to feel less guilty about not working. If I'm out for the day and just being present and enjoying it, I will be mad at myself for being lazy.

I knew it was bad when I would cancel hanging out with friends to go to work. I would lie, and say I had to do something else, like seeing a doctor, so they wouldn't question me.

My friends and family are all too aware of my addiction, so I have to hide it from them. It's like any addiction; you don't want people to know about it. Because they know it's not healthy.

My friends and family are also exhausted by my constant chat about work. It's all I really talk about. I have to actively work at not bringing everything back to work.

Why can't I be as addicted to exercise as I am to work?

I have prioritised work above everything. I have no hobbies, none. I am the definition of 'putting all your eggs in one basket'.

So, what should us workaholics do?

Be aware of it and proceed regardless?

Try to practise self-care?

Try to work less?

What I should do? I don't know. I really don't.

I think writing this has made me realise that maybe I do have a bigger problem than I thought.

I guess that, maybe, the first part of getting over an addiction is admitting you have one.

And . . . I admit it. I have a problem.

THE WORST THINGS EVER

- When you say goodbye to someone and keep running into them over and over again. So awkward.
- When you can't remember how you know someone.
- Shampoo and conditioner in one. This is not a thing. Stop trying to make this a thing.
- When your shellac manicure chips on day two. And the thing you got the shellac done for is on day three. FFS.
- When you get the middle seat on a 12-hour flight.
- Forgetting the lyrics to a song everyone is singing along to (and you should know the lyrics because you listen to that song all the time).
- When you try to pretend you haven't seen someone, and you lock eyes and neither of you wants to engage but you have to.
- Washing your hair. Ugh. Enough already.
- People at kiosks in shopping centres who are desperate to sell you things (usually beauty products and cleaning stuff) and you just want to keep walking and you feel awful.
- When someone knows your name and you don't know theirs.
- When you run into a colleague outside the office and neither of you knows how to wrap up the conversation.
- When the sun goes down on a Sunday.
- Getting your period on holiday.

X
IS FOR . . .

X-RATED

We're 24 letters in and I feel like I've been on my best beha-
viour for most of this book but I have to tell this story. It gets
a little bit rude. Eventually.

I'm a list maker. I know. I look, sound and kind of am a
raging hot mess. But I also love the shit out of a list.

Even worse: I make dream boards.

Most people think dream boards are like Pinterest, but real.
You know, like a Year Nine girl's English folder, collaged with
DOLLY magazine cut-outs and pictures of famous people,
exotic islands, amazing clothes.

Nope. I don't do that.

Here's what I do.

Every year, I get an A4 piece of paper (that I've stolen from work), sit down, and write with a permanent marker (also stolen from work) what I want to achieve that year. Then I Blu Tack (also stolen from work) the piece of paper to my bedroom wall and I look at it every day.

Okay, I know it sounds crazy, or, at the very least, just a bit dumb. But I've been doing this since 2011. And I've gotta tell you: it works. Everything that goes on the list gets done. People ask me all the time, 'What's your process?' Then they look at me like I have two heads when I say: 'Um, in January, I write down what I want to achieve and I stick the bit of paper up on my bedroom wall, so I see it every day, and then . . . I work my arse off to do all the things on the list.'

That's, seriously, all there is to it.

I think the magic is partly to do with being honest about what you want, and partly with the fact that you're writing down what you want and reminding yourself of it every day. It keeps you focused.

Once I tested my theory. I wrote *Toowoomba* on a piece of paper while I was living in Griffith. No shit, three months later I got a call asking if I'd like to move to Toowoomba.

Guys, this works. I swear by it.

Here's a pic of what I wrote down at the start of 2017. It basically all happened.

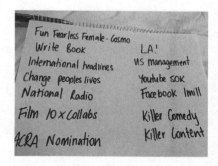

Fun Fearless Female - Cosmo
Write Book
International headlines
Change peoples lives
National Radio
Film 10 x Collabs
ACRA Nomination

LA!
US management
Youtube 50K
Facebook 1mill
Killer Comedy
Killer Content

I try to encourage other people to do the vision-board thing. My boyfriend told me recently he was feeling sad and unfocused—he wasn't where he wanted to be and was kind of floundering. So I told him to write a list, like I do. 'Write down what you want to achieve,' I told him. 'Stay accountable. Keep focusing. You'll get there.' He was really into it.

A day later, he told me he'd written it down, and I was so excited.

I walked upstairs to see a single word on a piece of paper that was stuck to the wall.

Anal.

I mean, it's not gunna happen. But now that it's on the wall . . .

X IS FOR SEXCUSES

(No. It's not. I know 'sexcuses' is not a word. And I know that even if it was, it would be listed under S, not X. But I didn't think through the fact that I'd have to write a chapter for X when I started this book, okay? So, let's carry on.)

Sex is always great when you get into a new relationship, isn't it? It's like Christmas when you're a kid and you really, really want a Barbie pool—the one with the little pump thing that makes waves in *real water*—and (!) *you actually get one*! You're so excited. You play with it *all the time*. You tell everyone how great it is.

But, after a while, the novelty wears off. The pool is fun, but do you have to play with it *all the time*? You have a life.

You need to do other stuff. You can't just sit around all day, pushing a tiny pump to see a tiny wave splash Barbie on her perfect face.

Is this metaphor working? I hope so.

My point is, after a while, sex just becomes . . . a chore. It's . . . ugh, do we have to? Eventually, I get to a point where I'm like: 'Right. We can have sex. But only if you do literally all of the work. And I literally mean I just want to lie there.'

So, whenever I don't feel like having sex (i.e. always), I have a little (long) list of *sexcuses* I like to use. Feel free to borrow.

- I have a UTI.
- It's too hot.
- It's too cold.
- It's not hot enough.
- It's not cold enough.
- My boobs hurt.
- My boobs are too sensitive.
- I feel fat today.
- I feel ugly.
- I don't want to be touched.
- I feel like we had sex last week.
- I might be sick and I don't want to make you sick.
- I have a headache.
- I went to the gym and it hurts (cardio is hardio).
- I just had a shower.
- My back hurts.
- My arms hurt.
- My legs hurt.

- My face hurts.
- I have to be up early.
- I'm on my period—I know, I've had it for four months; it *is* weird.
- I'm in a food coma.
- I've got that thing tomorrow. I definitely told you about it.
- My mum is next door.
- The neighbours might hear.
- The dog is watching.
- The cat is watching.
- We've run out of condoms (said while throwing a full box in the bin).
- I think I'm Christian now, so no sex before marriage. (Later you can denounce religion if you get really horny; I'm pretty sure God is fine with that.)
- I'm on a juice cleanse.
- I haven't waxed.
- I've just had laser.
- I had a manicure and I don't want to ruin it.
- I have to watch *RuPaul's Drag Race*.
- I'm already asleep.
- You smell.
- I smell.
- I feel like I need to poo.

Y
IS FOR . . .

YOUTH

They (old people) say youth is wasted on the young and I reckon that's completely true. While I don't think I wasted *my* youth, there are some things I'd like to go back and tell Teenage Tanya:

- Just because the sausage rolls are cheap at the canteen, that doesn't mean you need four of them.
- Do you know that boy you have a crush on? The one you've had a crush on for six years? The one who shares your deep love of the musicals *Rent* and *Wicked*? He's gay. He's *extremely* gay.

- I know you think you're being smart but, honestly, you do not need to save $700 to buy inflatable furniture for the house you'll live in as an adult. Trust me: it won't really take off.

- You will find this really hard to believe, but (truthbomb) Fila tracksuit pants—the kind with buttons down the side— are not attractive and never will be. Stop begging Mum for three pairs. Or any pairs.

- When you're at school discos, spend more time dancing and hanging out with your mates, and maybe even seeing if you can crack onto one of those boys you like (not the gay one: see above), and less time complaining to the canteen ladies about the lack of Wizz Fizz.

- Stop doing that thing where you ignore boys in your class but then run home to talk to them for hours and hours on MSN and ICQ. Just talk to them IRL.

- Listen to me: you are not as fat as you think you are. Actually, your body is amazing. Girl, you should be wearing a shorter skirt and a gold bikini at all times.

- Don't hang around shopping centres on Thursday nights. It's weird. (Why was this a thing?)

- Don't take this personally, but you will *always* fail the beep test in PE. You were born to sit, and sit you will.

- Impulse is not an antiperspirant.

- Lose the butterfly clips. All 40 of them, please.

- Don't straighten your hair with an iron. When you are 32, you'll still feel the scar tissue every day when you put your hair up in a ponytail.

- Always be yourself . . . even if it's difficult. Don't try so hard to fit in.

- The things you were bullied and teased about in high school will be the things people celebrate (and pay you for) when you're a grown-up.
- Oh, one more thing: buy shares in something called Facebook.

YOU KNOW YOU'RE OLD WHEN . . .

- You relate to the parents in movies. It's strange when you watch *The Little Mermaid* and when Ariel says, 'I'm 16, I'm not a child anymore!' you think: *Ariel, you have no idea what you're on about. You are a child. You have no idea what's going on, even though you think you do.* And then she keeps going, with 'But Daddy, I love him!' And you're looking for something to throw at the telly and thinking, *Bitch, you don't even KNOW him, you saw him ONCE, on a boat.*
- You complain about the price of things and use the phrase 'in my day'. This is super embarrassing, obviously, but *in my day* a coffee was not $6.50 (also back in my day, to be fair, coffee was International Roast and not, like, a large soy latte with a double shot and chai powder. I know. I am a wanker. Let's move on). As soon as those words come out of my mouth, though, all I can hear is my mum telling me off for asking for $2 to buy a bag of lollies from the corner store. She would look deep into my eyes with their sugar-craving expression, and say, 'Two dollars! For mixed lollies? Tanya Hennessy, you must be joking! In my day, for

sixpence you could buy a bag of mixed lollies, see a movie, get a haircut, and go to Fiji for five nights. And you'd still come home with change.' I am now that woman.

- You want practical gifts for Christmas and your birthday. Like a vacuum cleaner or a fuel voucher.
- You don't want to wear heels anymore.
- You think a big night means it finishes at 11 p.m.
- You don't really care about how you look, but are genuinely surprised at how gross you have let yourself become.
- Losing weight is hard.
- Hangovers are a near-death experience. It was so easy to bounce out of bed the next day when you were 21; at 32, you need life support.
- Something always hurts: neck, back, wrists . . . something.
- You think of uni as being four years ago but it was 10 years ago. That's confronting.
- You don't get what dabbing, or some acronym, means, and because you're worried you're old, you're constantly low-key googling things.
- You know you're old when you need a lot of notice before an event. When I was 18, I would need 20 minutes; in my 30s, I need nine months' notice before a party.
- You look for footwear that has upper-arch support.
- You have regular conversations about gardening.
- You call dubstep and house music 'noise'.
- You have a Thermomix. Or want a Thermomix.
- You've cancelled plans so you can do laundry. Or take a nap.
- You grunt while sitting down or getting up.
- People call you at 8 p.m. and ask, 'Did I wake you?'

- Your friend is pregnant and you say 'Congrats!' not 'Sorry!'
- You allocate time to do housework.
- You worry about being too far away from your house.

Being old is the best. But, while I love my 32-year-old brain, I miss my 18-year-old boobs. #gravelrash

Z

Z
IS FOR . . .

ZZZZZ

Is anyone else tired, like, all the time? I am. To all the mums and dads out there: I seriously don't know how you deal with the sleep deprivation. It's horrendous. I feel like I've done some seriously stupid stuff while tired . . .

- Bought a hot coffee and a cold bottle of water at a café and promptly chucked the soy latte in my handbag. Wisely, I kept the—closed—bottle of water in my hand. I'm smart like that.
- Tried to take my eye make-up off with nail polish remover.

- Put a carton of eggs in the dishwasher.
- Put flour in my coffee. It wasn't as good as sugar.
- Spread oil over a hot pan *with my finger*. Ten out of 10 would not recommend.
- Got a third-degree burn when I took a bowl of soup out of the microwave (that had been in there for nine minutes) without a tea towel over my hands. If we ever meet, ask me to show you the scar.
- Cried and screamed in a carpark because I thought I'd lost my car. It was at home. I'd actually taken the train in that day.
- Tried to pay for my groceries with my Medicare card. (Does not work.)
- Plugged my wallet into my phone charger. (Again, does not work.)
- Forgot I was on a plane and began singing along to the soundtrack of the musical *Dear Evan Hansen*. Ten out of 10 *would* recommend, but my fellow passengers probably would not.
- Ate soap. It's a long story.
- Drank liquid detergent. Now, that's a *really* long story.

EPILOGUE

So . . . that's my book.

Done. Finito. End scene.

I must say reading this back, I am stoked that so many Disney and massage anecdotes made their way into this book. Believe it or not, I had more. I was actually pushing for this book to be called *MASSAGE: A series of uncomfortable experiences I've had topless* and have the whole book full of massage stories. Also, there are a lot of stories about kids and parenting which I never would have imagined would be the case. Oh, and I talked about food a lot, which I did imagine.

When I started writing this book I didn't know how I would finish it. I kept asking myself *How will I know when it's finished?* then I realised . . . it's the alphabet. It's A to Z. *Woman, you'll be done when you hit Z.*

(Yet, here I am still writing post-Z . . .)

But in all seriousness, I'm not sure how to finish this book. My initial idea was to publish the nudes I sent Tom on Snapchat here because I looked good, but the publishers were like . . . 'Can we suggest rethinking this?'

So in lieu of nudes, my impulse was to google 'How to write an epilogue', 'How do you finish a book' and 'Examples of good endings of books'.

I guess that's a great indication of the theme of this book. Looking for someone who has done it before me to explain and tell me what to do. And me asking, 'Am I doing this right?'

The difference is, as I finish this book, I am finally able to answer my own question.

I *am* doing this right. I know I am. I can say this with zero self-doubt and 100 per cent assurance—which I'm sure after reading this you'll know is a big deal. I am doing it right . . . for me. This is what works for me—and that is enough. I don't need to ask Google, I don't need to ask anyone.

I know that what I am doing is right.

The most liberating part is that I don't care if I'm doing it wrong.

What a resolution.

I'm sad to finish this book because it feels as if a chapter of my life is over. It's closing. As I write this, I realise that things are changing for me. I can feel it.

I hope to have a child in the next few years (Ahhh!) and I know that if I'm fortunate enough for that to eventuate, soon things will be very different for me.

I'm scared to move away from this part of my life. I'm comfortable. But nothing great ever came from a comfort zone.

I genuinely never thought I would be writing that I want to have children (because of all the reasons listed in K is for Kids and all the parenting chapters). I never thought kids would be a part of my life. Ever. Yet, here I am. Excited at the thought, but mainly terrified. But you know what?

I'd rather be terrified and do it than be terrified and not do it.

(Solid ending.)

PS I can't wait to be pregnant. Eating for two and being able to sit heaps 'cause pregnant? Heaven.

Plus, I already own so many maternity clothes.

ACKNOWLEDGEMENTS

Firstly, I would like to thank my incredibly supportive parents, Jan and Kevin. Thank you for being so patient, loving and encouraging.

You have been my biggest cheerleaders, and my rocks. I wouldn't be here without you. You have travelled around the country to see every damn thing I have been in—including that nude production I did at uni. Sorry. That was a lot on the eyes.

You answer the phone when I call you in tears (which is every other day) and you have never asked me to be anything other than myself. Thank you for encouraging me to create. I am eternally grateful to you both. I hope one day to be half the parents you are to me.

I would also like to thank my boyfriend, Thomas Poole. You are an extraordinary human being. I know I was a nightmare putting together this book—and you supported me every step of the way. No one has loved me better than you. I love you.

To my Gran (Terry), Nanna (Patricia) and Pop (Jack)—when I didn't believe in myself, you always did. Thank you for telling me, in my darkest moments, I could do it. Pop—you mean more to me than you will ever know. Thank you for being my ultimate muse and inspiration.

To my closest friends—you're all so brilliant and I need you all so much. I can't do life without you. You're not my blood but I think of you as family. Amy Lochhead, Ashlea O'Sullivan, Mekelle Mills, Courtney and Ryan Turton, Jamie Winbank, Tom Whitaker and my cousin Anna Hennessy.

An epic thank you to Kelly Fagan, from Allen and Unwin, who answered my anxious/overthinky texts and emails at all hours and held my hand every step of the way. Kelly, you went above and beyond, sorry I made so many edits, right up to the final publishing deadline. I think you're magic.

Finally, I would like to thank **you**. Yes, you, who bought this book for supporting me. If you have ever listened to my radio show/podcast, watched a video or read my writing. I appreciate you. I love you. I do it for you. This book is dedicated to you.

And . . . sorry to anyone I have forgotten.